HOW TO FEED YOU
THE BE

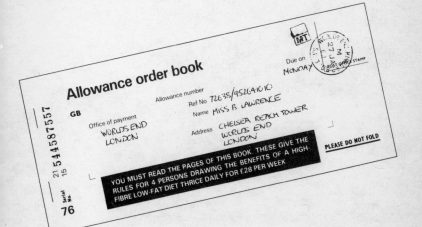

HOW TO FEED YOUR FAMILY
For £4 A Day

THE BENEFIT BOOK

BERNADINE LAWRENCE

THORSONS PUBLISHING GROUP

First published in 1989

British Library Cataloguing in Publication Data

Lawrence, Bernadine
How to feed your family for £4.00 a day
— the Benefit book
1. Food : Inexpensive dishes — Recipes
I. Title
641.5'52

ISBN 0–7225–1822–6

Photography by Pencil Point, Wellingborough, Northamptonshire

Published by Thorsons Publishers Limited, Wellingborough, Northamptonshire, NN8 2RQ, England.

Typeset by Burns & Smith, Derby
Printed in Great Britain by Richard Clay Limited, Bungay, Suffolk

1   3   5   7   9   10   8   6   4   2

Contents

Dedication

To Naughty Ned and Cuddly Cath, two of London's loveliest greengrocers.

Foreword

In the autumn of 1986 a letter to *The Times* aroused my interest. It described how at least one family, living in a high-rise council flat in an expensive part of London, ate well and healthily on supplementary benefit. I was in touch with Bernadine Lawrence at once.

Her idea of a book to help those in a similar position to her own family had not been well received by the groups dedicated to helping those caught in the poverty trap because they thought it might be used to depress the benefit and that is definitely not why this book was written. It is written with the principle in mind that a caring society should look after those who, through no fault of their own, are unable to be breadwinners.

How to Feed Your Family for £4.00 a Day is more, far more than a guide on how to eat cheaply. It is a return to basic good food made from the basic raw materials that so many have forgotten — or never been taught — how to use. It is the triumph of intelligent common sense over the problems of living on a low income.

In this book, Bernadine has reversed the trend towards highly packaged convenience foods that don't actually taste all that good or do you much good either and gone back to basics with, for example, the marvellous nutritive value of her splendid wholemeal loaf — a mainstay of the sound and economical nutrition of the Lawrence household, which comprises mum and dad plus four happy, healthy children aged between 15 months and 13 years.

Making just two meals for a family of four, you will recover the cost of the book and, from then on, you will profit both by saving money and through better health. *How to Feed Your Family for £4.00 a Day* should be in every home and I wish it every success.

MAURICE HANSSEN

Foreword

When I called on Bernie Lawrence and her young family in 1987 she was busy preparing a basket of fresh, home-cooked food for the children to take to the local Harvest Festival. Not for Bernie the traditional urban offering of a tin of rice pudding and a box of biscuits. She can't afford such things.

Although she has the advantage of living in fashionable Chelsea in a council flat overlooking the Thames that would fetch half a million if it were 'gentrified', Bernie is financially highly disadvantaged. Her sole income is a handout from the State and after paying for essentials, there's not much left over on which to feed six people healthily. She knew from experience that there wasn't much good health in costly packets and tins and heavily advertised 'convenience' foods. In any case, there wasn't enough money in her purse for that kind of stuff; every penny had to be made to count nutritionally.

Bernie's great achievement in feeding the family on £4 a day demonstrates that there *is* life beyond white sliced bread, frozen burgers, oven-fried chips and toffees. Bernie may be bobbing about on the poverty line but she has no intention of drowning.

Over the years she has devised a wide repertoire of meals which cost very little, are simple to prepare and full of goodness. This is healthy food, full of taste and flavour. It may be cheap but it's very, very cheerful. The recipes in *How to Feed Your Family for £4.00 a Day* are a survival manual for those caught in the poverty trap. But the book is more than that — if gastronomy means an intelligent and creative use of the best raw materials at your disposal then this is a distinguished exercise in gastronomy and triumphant proof that the art of eating well can be the prerogative of the poor as well as the well-heeled.

DEREK COOPER

Introduction

What exactly, you may ask, is the Benefit Book? The Benefit Book is a step-by-step guide written for all: for the student struggling to get by on an impossible grant, for the former city whizz kid in post-crash Britain, for the thrifty fellow from the Inland Revenue who feels that the wife is overspending, in fact for anybody who would like to eat well, like their family to do so while keeping a little money in their pocket, but above all, the Benefit Book is for the total non-cook faced with the prospect of an existence on the Benefit. Its objective is to show you how to feed well a family of four thrice daily on a high-fibre, low-fat diet for no more than £28 per week with all the recipes costed.

But what is a high-fibre, low-fat diet, you may ask? Something for health freaks, some of you may suspect. But not at all! Don't let yourself be put off by mention of a diet just because you know you have a hearty appetite. On the contrary, the Benefit Book will show many of you how to indulge to a level you probably wouldn't have achieved had you spent twice as much, and what's more you'll probably be a lot healthier for it.

What then is fibre? Fibre is something that many of us would benefit from eating more of. Fibre is the name for the indigestible part of cereals, fruit or vegetables. Therefore, all fibrous foods originate from the earth. There is no fibre in animal produce such as eggs, cheese, meat or fish, yet fibre is crucial to everyone's good health. This fibre is essential to anyone's diet if their bowels are to be able to function properly. Yet much of our modern food is put through processes which simply strip it of its most fibrous parts and result in a defective product. But a growing number of people are turning to foods which have not been processed in such ways. These are known as wholefoods and, though available for some years but only in specialist shops usually health shops which many think of as rather cranky, now wholefoods are becoming available in many major supermarkets, certain such stores even having their own brands of wholefoods.

Of course your greengrocer has always had an excellent range of wholefoods available but unfortunately just like the manufacturers, countless people go and needlessly strip their purchases from the greengrocer of the most fibrous parts — a process known as peeling. But wherever possible, my advice to you is either to scrub or to scrape your vegetables till clean and retain the peel, thus retaining the maximum of their fibre though, owing to regional factors such as lead pollution or certain chemical fertilizers, that should be a thorough scrubbing. Also no fibrous foods will lose any of this fibre whatever the method of cooking you use to prepare them. Unfortunately, many tend to think only of relatively expensive purchases from their greengrocer as high in fibre such as asparagus, avocodos or Chinese lettuce and remain unaware that potatoes and carrots or even a couple of slices of wholemeal toast with a good helping of baked beans from the local supermarket are an excellent source of fibre. Any diet that is naturally high in its fibre content will help to prevent any problems with your bowels, in fact visits to the loo become a regular routine and constipation a thing of the past on a naturally fibrous diet like that offered in the Benefit Book.

But just what (do I hear you asking?) upon what is that most sensational claim based — the claim that it is quite feasible for four persons to eat well while all grocery expenditure is kept within the seemingly crazy sounding figure of only £28 per week? What this claim is based upon is over half a decade's worth of first-hand experience as a recipient of state benefits and feeding well a young family all throughout upon just that sum — an average of £4 per day. The costs given in the Benefit Book for the many ingredients required should be taken as approximates, of course, but are based upon the highest price I can recall having paid for them and living as I have throughout those years atop a council block in Chelsea, overlooking a neighbourhood with one of the highest concentrations of millionaires in the land, this has not been achieved in a locality exactly well known for low-prices. Thus, if it's possible in Chelsea it should be possible anywhere!

I can still recall clearly the sense of come-down several years ago, realizing that I would have to rely upon state hand-outs in order to manage, to survive, and the prospect seemed harrowing.

The entire episode was an over-ridingly depressing affair. I distinctly remember going along to the local DHSS to wait in a smoke-filled room, which remained dingy despite the bright sunshine outside, to be interviewed — an event which, when it finally occurred, was extremely brief and at a time long after that on my appointment card — only to return home and await delivery of a letter informing me of my entitlements — that was just how much (or how little) I was to be expected to live on. I was all too aware of reports in the media that payment levels set by the DHSS were inadequate, simply not enough to live on, but nothing had prepared me for the figures on that letter when it did fall in my door. Opening it up to discover the details of my income, what I would have to manage on, I can recall, was a come-down on top of a come-down.

In the initial weeks on the Benefit it proved simply impossible to make the pittance issued every Monday at my local Post Office last the 7 days for which it was intended. Nights were spent awake trying to envisage the future after the gas, the electricity and the telephone had been discontinued, as seemed a certainty. If I couldn't buy groceries for the week, how would I pay those inevitable quarterlies? In my former years I had acquired costly eating habits either buying take-away's or eating out. I was a total non-cook. The most inventive of my edible creations were open-sandwiches consisting of either cooked meat or fish garnished with fresh salad upon thick slices of wholemeal bread. But suddenly even a loaf of wholemeal bread was expensive, too expensive for me to buy every other day!

Thus I considered making my own wholemeal bread. The flour and yeast were available in the local supermarket, I had received bread tins among other accessories to my cooker some years before and bread had been the first recipe I had ever tackled in a domestic science lesson at school, and with pleasing results, I might add. So if I could make it then, why not now? Henceforth home-baked wholemeal bread became a cornerstone of my family's diet and probably the first of my Basic Essentials and is, therefore, a major ingredient in the recipe to eating well on the Benefit.

As time progressed and my standard of bread baking improved, so my small repertoire of recipes grew and I found myself no longer fearing but positively enjoying my task of cooking; that is deriving a sense of satisfaction from my daily preparations, which would vary according to their quality. In other words — a good meal brought a good reaction from my family and all would retire content, myself included. This helped to give each day some purpose and to provide some alternative to the awful sense of idleness which can, otherwise, strike anybody made redundant and suddenly deprived both of a function to fulfil and of the resources required to pursue other activities leisurely or otherwise.

The considerable savings, also, suddenly made possible through the low cost of my own cooking, enabled me to achieve a weekly surplus, having kept all grocery expenditure within £28 per week. Only a small surplus by many people's standards, now in this age of such low rates of income tax, but quite a contrast to my earliest days spent unemployed, on the Benefit and worried by seemingly unstoppable debts. Also, having stretched £28 so far, one starts to look at the remaining surplus as capable of doing more than one would have previously expected of it.

But also, living upon a high-density, inner city council development, naturally, I met with other young parents in situations similar to my own initial dilema, that is in receipt of state benefits and not able to find ways to cope and stretch their miniscule incomes far enough to meet their many financial responsibilities. One main factor in their difficulties, much to their surprise, did not occupy a prominent position in my own living room: this, of course, was a TV set. Time and time again, it became apparent, when in conversation with such persons, having perhaps asked them to dinner, that their own inadequate and costly menus back home were by-products, largely, of commercials pumped out of their unrestrained TV sets, inevitably leading vulnerable youngsters to apply pressure on their parents for what can only be honestly described as 'junk food', and time and again such persons were amazed upon learning of the low cost of the substantial and largely fresh meal to which they were sitting down and, indeed, eager to know just how to prepare such meals for their own youngsters, who were, on the whole, overfed and undernourished. I, in turn would be only too glad to give them the recipe for the meal, usually written out last thing in pencil, for them to take home.

But still, week in, week out, while I queued to make my exit through the check-out at the local supermarket, it was all too often apparent just whose shopping and eating habits were dictated by the TV commercials, their bags and boxes piled high with so-called 'convenience foods', either packaged in costly tin containers, or to be rushed home to keep in costly deep freezes, operation of which only further increased their electricity bills. Unfortunately, these persons were the very persons who could least afford the excessive cost of such products forming the bulk of their diet but knew no better and so ate at a high cost, both to their purses and to their health.

It was, however, only upon reading a most upsetting feature some time later in a certain national daily, about the problem of malnourishment among many youngsters, not in any Third World country but here in our own backyard in good old Britain, that I felt compelled to do something on a larger scale to help such people, having felt trapped once myself in the belief that I had not enough available to get my family and myself through each week, not knowing that there was a way through the food maze, as a result of ignorance, never really having been taught the facts about food. I wished simply to get my own still relatively small selection of recipes out to those whose children, through their poor diets, could not eat well enough to remain healthy and who, subsequently, became a greater burden on the state. In order to do this, I wrote to the director of a major anti-poverty pressure-group which had participated in the feature, extensively providing many of the facts and data. What I suggested was that they published either a diet card or sheet upon which there should be seven of my recipes for main meals: that is something different for each day of the week and a smaller number of recipes for breakfasts and lunches, with all ingredients costed and all attainable within £28 per week. The response of the group's director was to point out that were such information put out by themselves certain politicians would seize upon it to use as hard evidence that Benefit levels were abundant, a truly paradoxical catch-22 situation and, although flabbergasted by the response, I have never doubted the sincerity of the reasons given.

But, several years on, and my range of recipes has multiplied, as has Britain's number of have-nots. For many people things have simply gone from bad to worse and when mention of this episode was made in letter to *The Times*, such was the flood of requests from readers, asking for the recipes, that it was beyond my limited resources to reply to all. But when readers of *The Times* write en masse asking how to manage on £28 per week, the need for the Benefit Book is there! But, having said that, I do have a question to ask of any smart politician who may wish to wield the Benefit Book in such a way, and that is, quite simply, do you and your family manage on £28 per week? For any man who quoteth the Benefit Book should live by the Benefit Book!

1
Basic Essentials

Items contained in this section are either whole recipes which will prove very useful in keeping your diet both cheap and healthy or preparations which you will find essential when making many of the other recipes throughout the Benefit Book and, lastly, one utility which I have found crucial in preparation of many of those recipes.

Note on Measuring

The most accurate way of measuring with a spoon is to use level measures, that is, level off to the top of the spoon with a knife. (A heaped spoon can contain anything from two to four times as much as a level spoon.)

A pinch = $\frac{1}{4}$ teaspoon
2 teaspoons = 1 dessertspoon
2 dessertspoons = 1 tablespoon
25g/1oz flour = 1 heaped tablespoon
25g/1oz sugar = 1 level tablespoon

In our household we prefer to measure ingredients using cups. Conveniently, one of our cups holds 285ml/$\frac{1}{2}$ pint of liquid, thus a measuring jug, filled to the 285ml/$\frac{1}{2}$ pint mark, can serve ideally when measuring out cupfuls. For those of you who feel that cup measurements would be a lot easier to use, I have listed below some of the staple ingredients used in this book and their amounts per cup.

Beans — 1cup = 165g/5$\frac{1}{2}$ oz
Cornmeal — 1 cup = 140g/5 oz
Flour — 1 cup = 115g/4 oz
Lentils — 1 cup = 165g/5$\frac{1}{2}$ oz

Macaroni — 1 cup = 140g/5 oz
Milk powder — 1 cup = 115g/4 oz
Porridge oats — 1 cup = 115g/4 oz
Raisins — 1 cup = 140g/5 oz
Rice — 1 cup = 165g/5½ oz
   Cooked — 1 cup = 170g/6 oz
Rolled oats — 1 cup = 115g/4 oz
Sugar — 1 cup = 170g/6 oz
Sultanas — 1 cup = 140g/5 oz

In fact, any need for such elaborate machinery as weighing scales (the dread of many a non-cook) can be avoided altogether simply by taking note of the quantities in which foods are bought and dividing them appropriately. For example, when making a pastry case for a Quick Quiche simply cut half (or just under half) off a 250g/9 oz block of margarine, and when making Bargain Bread use all but one-tenth of a 1.5kg/3lb 5 oz bag of wholemeal flour, and the only instruments required are a knife and a bowl.

A Typical Weekly Shopping List

3 bags wholemeal flour	£1.59
1 tin dried yeast	55
1 roasting chicken	£2.50
225g/½ lb Cheddar cheese	70
Large tin baked beans	58
Tube tomato purée	26
1lb 2 oz/500g red split lentils	49
1lb 2 oz/500g wholewheat spaghetti	49
455g/1lb brown rice	52
1lb 2oz/500g blackeye beans	59
115g/4 oz mackerel pâté	55

> ● The purchasing of 'Home Brands' in supermarkets not only reduces your weekly shopping bill but also offers a greater choice, e.g., wholewheat spaghetti, soya margarine, sea-salt etc. Also, supermarket 'Home Brands' are usually the same products in different packaging and at a lower price.

115g/4 oz humous	45
2 tubs (1 kg/2lb 3 oz) soya margarine	84
2 tins pilchards	52
1¾ pints/1 litre vegetable oil	49
1lb 2 oz/500g sea salt	35
2lb 3 oz/1kg demerara sugar	73
2 fillets of mackerel	£1.50
1 tin tomatoes	20
4 litres/7 pints milk (milk token)	
12 eggs	90
2 bottles concentrated apple juice	£2.77
225g/8 oz coffee/chicory	89
4.1kg/9lb potatoes	90
1.4k/3lb onions	60
Garlic	20
455g/1lb carrots	20
455g/1lb sprouts	30
1 marrow	30
1 cauliflower	50
3 sweetcorns	60
115g/4 oz mushrooms	25
1 green pepper	25
3 lettuces	90
455g/1lb tomatoes	45
1 cucumber	40
3 bunches watercress	90
1 celery	40
900g/2 lb apples	70
1 lemon	10
Bunch bananas	60
6 oranges	42
1 grapefruit	20
455g/1lb pears	35
Total	£27.98

> ● Use the plastic bags available at the fruit and vegetable counters in supermarkets to hold spillable items such as flour, sugar, rice etc. These have other uses at home — storing bread etc.

Bargain Bread

Baking your own bread! The idea no doubt sounds far-fetched, impractical, possible for some others, perhaps, but not for yourself. But if you consider that it takes only 20 minutes (yes 20!) to prepare 2 large wholemeal loaves (10 minutes per loaf) for around 33p each. That is probably less time than many of you are now willing to spend making an excursion, in all weathers, to pay twice as much for a grossly defective product handled by who knows how many and never with the same care as one's own bread. Is the idea really all that far-fetched when one discovers just how quick and easy a process making wholemeal bread is? All that seems far-fetched is that so few people do so.

Your family will love it and love you for it. Not only does baking one's own wholemeal bread increase the bread in your shopping purse and the nourishment in your diet, but your own morale will rise every time, along with the dough in your oven. My own loaves have brought some most touching compliments and from a wide assortment of people ranging from fellow-claimants to somebody with a bank balance nine figures long.

It is no coincidence that in our terminology money became increasingly referred to as dough or bread until the mass of people adopted these terms for common usage and they became forever woven into the language. Both these references have come about because of the significance of bread in our diet. Since time immemorial, from the instance that tribes chanted and prayed to their Gods to make their grain crops abundant so that they need never go short of bread, to the present when its very primacy still necessitates its inclusion in the Lord's Prayer, bread in all its many forms has been an important dietary staple for all nations. Technically speaking we have come a long way since say Roman Times but, paradoxically, their diet was superior to ours simply because the mass of people ate wholegrain bread. Our modern civilization has taken a huge step backwards in mass-producing bread stripped of its nutrients — the germ and the bran.

Grain is composed of three elements — the germ, the endosperm and the bran. The germ contains protein, thiamine, iron, riboflavin, niacin and vitamin E. The endosperm contains a little protein but is mainly carbohydrates. The bran is the protective coating around the grain and contains iron and B vitamins. Most people today in the West, in spite of the growing trend towards wholegrain bread still eat bread which contains little more than starch and it is impossible for the manufacturers to replace all the nutrients destroyed in the milling process. Bargain Bread is made from wholemeal flour and contains 100 per cent of the wheat grain. Not only is Bargain Bread high in fibre, it is also high in nourishment. This may be bread-line Britain, but this is bloody good bread!

Bargain Bread

Ingredients   *Approximately*
850ml/1½ pints water
15ml/1 level tablespoon sugar
30ml/6 teaspoons dried yeast (Allinson's)   11p
1.4kg/3 lb wholemeal flour   55p
10ml/2 level teaspoons salt

Method
1   Turn oven onto its lowest heat and leave to warm. Heat water
    until hand hot, slightly above blood heat (about 55°C/110°F).
    Dissolve the sugar in 60ml/4 tablespoons water, add the yeast
    and leave in a warm place to froth, 10 minutes approximately.
2   Measure flour and salt into a bowl. Add the yeast mixture then
    gradually add the rest of the water. Mix to a dough and knead
    for 10 – 15 minutes, adding more flour if necessary to make a
    dough that is smooth, elastic and not sticky. (With practice, the
    mixing bowl should be left quite clean.)
3   Grease and flour 2 large loaf tins. Halve the dough and place in
    the bread tins.
4   Switch off the oven and leave the dough inside for approxi-
    mately 30 minutes or until the mixture has risen 2.5cm/1 inch
    above the rim of the tins.
5   Bake at 200°C/400°F (Gas Mark 6) for 40 minutes until brown
    on top.
6   Lastly, stand the loaves to cool on the wire rack from your grill.
    This will prevent them becoming too moist underneath.

Approximate cost of ingredients: 66p

- Bread — add a small amount of oil (1–2 tablespoons) to the dough to avoid too many crumbs
  when slicing. Alternatively, keep the bread crumbs
  for use in burgers and stuffings, etc.

Variations

Bread Buns

If short of suitable tins for making loaves, bread buns are quick and practical. Follow the recipe and method for Bargain Bread. Take half the kneaded dough and shape 10 bread buns. Place them on a greased baking sheet and leave them to rise in a warm place for 15–20 minutes or until they are twice their size. Bake on a low shelf of the oven for 25–30 minutes.

Bread Dough Dumplings

Simply separate $\frac{1}{4}$ of the dough ($\frac{1}{2}$ a loaf's worth) when making Bargain Bread and place in a plastic bag in the refrigerator until ready to use. Shape into about 12 small balls and roll each one in flour. Drop them into fast boiling salted water, cover with a lid and boil quickly for about 10 minutes. Lift the dumplings out of the water with a draining spoon and add the dumplings to stews or casseroles just before serving. Or serve them as a sweet with honey, jam or fruit.

- Bread storage: when cool store bread in clean plastic bags tied tightly. This keeps the bread remarkably fresh.

Raisin Bread

Ingredients   *Approximately*
30–45ml/2–3 level tablespoons brown sugar   8p
850ml/1½ pints water (heated to 55°C/110°F)
30ml/6 teaspoons dried yeast   11p
1.4kg/3 lb wholemeal flour   55p
2.5ml/½ level teaspoon salt
275g/10 oz raisins   44p
60ml/4 tablespoons vegetable oil (optional)
Optional egg wash of 1 egg beaten with 15ml/1 tablespoon brown
    sugar and 30ml/2 tablespoons milk

Method
1 Dissolve the sugar in 140ml/¼ pint of hot water, add yeast and
   leave to froth for 10 minutes.
2 Mix the flour, salt and raisins and pour into the yeast mixture.
   Knead and gradually add the rest of the water with the oil.
3 Continue as for Bargain Bread and if liked, brush the loaf with
   egg wash before baking.

Approximate cost of ingredients: £1.18

Of course mistakes can be made when baking one's own bread
and such mistakes are most likely to occur in the initial attempts
when you are least familiar with the routine. Therefore, hopefully,
a brief reading of these guidelines prior to a first try at baking
bread may help avert any of the three most common mistakes
which might otherwise have had discouraging effects.

Firstly, in my own experience, the most common mistake has
been to stand the yeast after mixing it to rise in an over-heated
oven. Secondly, if the water used when mixing the yeast is too hot
the result will be the same — the yeast will, in effect, be killed and
will not rise (form a frothy head). If after some 10–15 minutes the
yeast fails to rise it should be discarded for some fresh yeast; if it
is not replaced then one is preparing 2 very heavy loaves destined
not to rise. If, however, your yeast produces a fine head and is
mixed successfully into a dough, then avoid the third and final

downfall and do not stand the dough to rise in an over-warm oven, as this will have the same effect upon the yeast at this stage and your dough will not rise (expand) to produce large loaves.

But even if one of these mistakes is made at some point and the dough never rises, the outcome will just be smaller, heavier loaves which is only a cosmetic failure and in no way are such loaves deficient in terms of nourishment. So, on such occasions, I strongly recommend you to do as I have and consume such bread perhaps with a soup or in a bread and butter pudding, or simply cut into small cubes and served with warm milk and dried fruit and, of course, to try again!

The Humble Spud

The humble spud, as we tend to think of it today, was not always so humble. Only four centuries earlier and the potato was quite a delicacy in Europe and grown only in the gardens of the rich, having been fetched by Spaniards from its homeland high in the Andes in South America where it had long been cultivated. It tended to be eaten at rich and privileged tables as a separate starter to meals, rather like an avocado today.

But come the Industrial Revolution and the status of the potato changed as its potential to feed large numbers of people cheaply was realized until, by the middle of the eighteenth century, potatoes had replaced bread as the main foodstuff of more than half of the population. Methods of preparing the humble spud have, naturally, increased since then, some proving phenomenal (try to envisage Britain without all of its fish and chip shops or kids without potato crisps), but the demise of the humble spud in my view came with the advent of so-called instant mashed potatoes, when the vegetable was skinned and reduced to a colourless, flavourless pulp and sold in sachets bearing claims that the addition of measured volumes of boiling water would produce delicious mashed potatoes in seconds. I am still of the opinion that somebody ought to have challenged this claim under the Trade Descriptions Act.

Potatoes you will find, because of their potential for cheap nourishment, are an important component of many of my meals in the Benefit Book and are, therefore, indeed a Basic Essential but, despite this, I have no use for a potato peeler, the reason being that the removal of the skin from a potato would amount to the complete waste of a most beneficial part. This is because most of potato's fibre is in the skin and therefore, whether baking, boiling or roasting them, I use a small plastic pan-scrub to wash off excess dirt from any such vegetables. Then after scrubbing I remove any eyes or bad parts with a kitchen knife, retaining the maximum of the potato's fibre, calcium and vitamin C.

Baked Potatoes

Baking is by far my most frequent method of preparing potatoes. This is because (besides the fact I simply find baked potatoes delicious) I often use the oven to prepare the main part of the meal and a vacant top shelf inside will accommodate a large trayful of spuds and save the use of a top burner. This not only helps towards smaller gas bills but also reduces the chance of accidents in that often hectic pre-dinner period. The baked potato is also the humble spud cooked in its most wholesome form with none of the goodness lost in water which is then poured away.

Method
1 Simply wash each potato and remove any bad parts.
2 Bake on a top shelf at 200°C/400°F (Gas Mark 6) for 45 minutes.
3 Serve with margarine, salt and freshly ground black pepper.

Roast Potatoes

Ingredients   *Approximately*
900g/2 lb potatoes   20p
85g/3 oz margarine or 45ml/3 tablespoons vegetable oil   9p
Salt and freshly ground black pepper

Method
1 Wash, scrub and, if necessary, eye potatoes (remove any bad parts). Cut them in half and place them with fat in a baking tin (or around the roast) and roast them in a hot oven (220°C/425°F, Gas Mark 7) 45 minutes.
2 When they are partially cooked, turn them over so that they brown on both sides.
3 Season with salt and freshly ground pepper 5 minutes before serving.

Approximate cost: 29p

Boiled Potatoes

Ingredients   *Approximately*
900g/2 lb new potatoes   40p

Method
1 Scrub the potatoes lightly and chop them into halves or quarters, depending on their size.
2 Cook them in boiling, salted water for about 15 minutes until tender but firm. Drain and serve.
3 Alternatively cook with parsley, mint or chopped chives.

Approximate cost: 40p

Cheese Stuffed Potatoes

Ingredients	*Approximately*
900g/2 lb potatoes	20p
225g/8 oz grated Cheddar	70p
85g/3 oz margarine or butter	9p
Salt and freshly ground black pepper	

Method
1 Wash, scrub, eye and stab potatoes. Place them in a hot oven (220°C/425°F/Gas Mark 7) on a baking tray or tin and bake for 45 minutes until cooked. (Test by inserting a fork to find out if they are tender inside.)
2 Remove potatoes from the oven and cut them in half. Scoop out the cooked potato, mash and combine with the cheese and margarine.
3 Season with salt and freshly ground black pepper and fill the potato cases with the mix. Return to the oven and continue to bake for 10 –15 minutes until golden brown on top. Serve with salad etc.

Approximate cost: 99p

Creamed Potatoes

Ingredients	*Approximately*
900g/2 lb potatoes	20p
55–85g/2–3 oz margarine or butter	9p
Salt and freshly ground black pepper	

Method
1 Wash, scrub and eye potatoes. Chop them up small and boil for 10 –15 minutes until tender.
2 Drain the potatoes, the mash them. Add the margarine and blend in thoroughly.
3 Season to taste with salt and freshly ground black pepper.

Approximate cost: 29p

Potato Fritters

Ingredients	*Approximately*
900g/2 lb cooked potatoes, mashed	20p
30ml/2 level tablespoons breadcrumbs	
5 eggs	40p
10ml/2 level teaspoons tomato purée	
Crushed garlic, to taste	5p
45–60ml/3–4 tablespoons vegetable oil	5p

Method
1 Mix all the ingredients and season with salt and freshly ground black pepper.
2 Shape into flat cakes and fry in a little oil until brown on both sides. Alternatively, brown in oven in an oiled tray.

Approximate cost: 70p

Saucy Potatoes

Ingredients	Approximately
900g/2 lb potatoes	20p
55–85g/2–3 oz streaky bacon, cubed	24p
1 large onion, finely chopped	10p
30ml/2 level tablespoons flour	
570ml/1 pint milk	26p
A little grated nutmeg	

Method
1 Wash, scrub and eye the potatoes. Cut them in half and boil them until tender for about 15 minutes.
2 Drain and cut them into thick slices while they are still hot.
3 Return the potatoes to the pan, cover and keep them warm on the cooker.
4 Fry the bacon, add the onion and continue to cook until golden.
5 Add the flour and gradually add the milk. Stir well and bring to the boil.
6 Season with salt and pepper then combine the potatoes with the sauce. Stir and simmer together briefly. Serve hot.

Approximate cost of ingredients: 80p

Brown Rice

Brown rice is a Basic Essential in this book because it can be included in so many recipes and is an excellent source of roughage (fibre) and nutrients. The cultivation of brown rice and other grain crops which were easily grown, high-yielding and storable was a major event in the founding of modern civilization, for only with a dependable food supply readily available were countless tribes able to stop their wanderings in search of food, and settle down.

Brown rice is a still a Basic Essential for many people around the world, but highly milled and polished white rice is favoured in the West. Sadly, Third World countries are following suit and eating more white rice — a highly dangerous exercise for many dependent on rice who, as a result, develop Beri Beri (due to B vitamin loss) and die in their thousands.

Indeed, in many countries brown rice is left for the poor whilst the rich and fashionable eat white rice in adundance. This point was emphasized recently when speaking with a Malaysian friend. She happened to mention that she was on a diet and had cut out rice totally, a task which was particularly difficult, she stressed, as rice was a staple food in her country and formed the basis of many of her favourite meals.

'No, rice isn't fattening!' I declared (foolishly thinking she was referring to brown rice).

'It is!' she protested. Then when I started to extol the virtues of brown rice she screwed up her face. 'That's just for the poor people!' she exclaimed, and would not entertain the idea at all. Such is the social stigma of brown rice for many.

So here we have another paradox where the poor, who cannot afford the highly polished white rice, eat instead, brown rice which is far superior, whilst the rich and affluent who buy the highly esteemed white rice, eat an inferior produce.

White rice is grossly deficient because it has had the bran and the germ removed. The bran and the germ contain 80 per cent of the thiamine (vitamin B_1), whereas the endosperm, though constituting 90 per cent of the weight, contains less than 10 per cent of the thiamine. Also, research has shown that certain cardiac conditions and heart disease are related to thiamine deficiency — little wonder that heart disease is such a major killer in the West.

It is important to remember that rice washed in water too thoroughly loses some of the B vitamins, which are dissolved out. Similarly, if rice is boiled in excess water a considerable proportion of the B vitamins are likely to be discarded in the water after the rice has been cooked. Rice should therefore, always be cooked in just the amount of water it will absorb. Any water left over should be used for soup or stew, since it will contain valuable B vitamins which should not be wasted.

● Keep cooked rice, if unused, to make salads more substantial.

Brown Rice

Ingredients   *Approximately*
300g/11 oz brown rice   40p
1.1 litres/2 pints water
5ml/1 teaspoon salt

Method
1 Bring rice to boil in salted water. Let simmer for 5 minutes without lid then cover and cook on a low heat for about 15 minutes until soft and chewy, but not mushy.
2 To test, stick a knife in the rice and if starting to stick to the bottom of the pan and the knife emerges with cooked grains stuck to it, it's ready!
3 If the rice is almost cooked and there's plenty of liquid in the pan, cook with the lid off until the liquid has evaporated, or drain (saving the liquid!) and cook.
4 If the rice is not cooked but is sticking to the pan bottom, add about 150ml/5 fl oz of water, cover and cook until ready.

Approximate cost of ingredients: 40p

Red Kidney Beans

It is necessary to cook red kidney beans thoroughly or they will cause grave stomach upsets. It is also important to remember not to add any salt to the beans until they are cooked or they may never become tender. For most recipes bring 455g/1 lb of beans to the boil in 1.1 litres/2 pints water. Let boil vigorously for 10 minutes, then tip away the water, cover completely with fresh boiling water, and simmer on a low heat for 2 hours until tender. Test and, if still hard in the centre, cook for a further 30 minutes, adding more water if necessary. I like to cook mine until quite mushy after the starch grain has burst and the water has become sauce-like.

Blackeye Beans

For most recipes bring 455g/1 lb of beans to boil in 850ml/1½ pints water. Cover and simmer gently for 30 minutes. Season after the beans have cooked.

Red-Split Lentils

For use in soups 455g/1 lb of lentils will suffice for 1.1 litres/2 pints of water. Bring to the boil, being careful not to let it boil over as it forms quite a frothy head. Cover and simmer gently for 30 minutes.

For use in flans and loaves measure 340g/¾lb of lentils to 680ml/24 fl oz water. Simmer gently without covering, stirring occasionally, for 20–30 minutes until soft and firm. If the lentils are runny cook over a high heat, stirring constantly until firmer. Add a drop more water if the lentils are dry but not cooked and simmer until ready.

Sweet Corn

Corn is another member of the grain family, though it is often served as a vegetable. You can be sure it's high in fibre!

- Keep a jar or bottle for all leftover liquids from cooking vegetables or gravy or juices from the cooking of meat. This makes excellent stock for sauces or stews and will keep in the fridge for 5–6 days.

Corn on the Cob

Shuck the corn by removing the leafy wrapping and the thready corn silks. Drop in boiling water and cook for 10–15 minutes. Alternatively, boil in milk and water using ordinary milk or powdered. Serve with butter, salt and pepper, soy sauce etc.

Corn on the cob may also be baked in the oven. Leave the shucks on to retain moisture, and bake for 15–20 minutes in a moderate oven 180°C/350°F (Gas Mark 4). When the outer leaves are beginning to turn brown, it's ready. Peel back the shucks or just pull them off. Pull the silks off the end and serve. This method retains flavour and nutrients lost in boiling.

To remove corn kernels (cooked or raw) from the cob, stand the corn upright in a wide bowl and, holding the upper end, cut downwards along the cob. Delicious in soups, salads and pies etc.

Cornmeal

Besides use in porridge, puddings and cakes, cornmeal is very good in savoury recipes. Use 140g/5 oz of fine cornmeal to 680ml/24 fl oz of milk or water, 10ml/2 teaspoons salt and 30g/1 oz margarine or butter. Bring ingredients to the boil and simmer gently, stirring occasionally.

Corncakes

Ingredients	Approximately
1 egg	8p
200ml/7 fl oz milk	9p
140g/5 oz fine cornmeal	7p
115g/4 oz canned fish	26p
Salt and freshly ground black pepper	

Method
1 Beat the egg and milk and stir in the remaining ingredients.
2 Drop the batter by spoonfuls onto a well-oiled, pre-heated

frying pan. Cook over a moderate heat until crisp and golden
on both sides, turning only once.
3   Serve hot with salad garnish.

Approximate cost of ingredients: 50p

Popcorn

Method
1   Heat 30ml/2 tablespoons oil in a pan with tight fitting lid.
2   Add 30ml/2 tablespoons popcorn, cover and cook over a
    moderate heat until corn stops popping.
3   Sprinkle with salt and serve.

Approximate cost of ingredients: 10p

Pastries

Some people are wary about using wholemeal flour in pastries.
They find it grainy and heavy, by comparison to the talcum-
powder-like flour they've been used to. Often when it comes to
rolling it out it breaks and doesn't hold in one piece. Then, to top it
all, after baking, it seems so hard and crunchy by comparison to
white flour. But it's merely a matter of becoming accustomed to
the difference and appreciating the superiority of wholemeal
flour!

Once you have kneaded a good dough — not too sticky or not
too dry, you should find it comparatively easy to roll out. If the
dough crumbles when rolling out — don't panic, knead it again
with a drop more water. If the dough is too sticky, add a little more
flour. Even if, after rolling out, the dough starts to fragment when
rollling it back on the pin ready to place in the flan tin — don't
despair, place what remains on the rolling pin in the flan tin and
mould on the rest after moistening it a little. After lining the tin with
the pastry, if you seem a little short of dough use the trimmings
from around the edge of the tin to patch the pastry case. And if
you are still a little short — no sweat, the pastry-case will be a
little uneven but taste just as nice!

- Keep surplus pastry in a plastic bag in the fridge. It will keep for 5–6 days.

Flan Pastry

Ingredients   **Approximately**
115g/4 oz margarine *or* 90ml/3fl oz vegetable oil   12p/4p
225g/½ lb wholemeal flour   8p
A little cold water or milk

Method
1 Rub the margarine into the flour until the mixture resembles fine breadcrumbs. Add a little cold water or milk and knead into a dough.
2 Roll the pastry out evenly on a floured surface. Use to line the flan case (rolling the pastry up onto the rolling pin and unrolling it over the tin).
3 Prick all over the base of the flan with a fork. Partially bake at 170°C/325°F (Gas Mark 3) for 10 minutes.

Approximate cost: 20p

Crumbly Pastry (for pies and pasties)

Ingredients   **Approximately**
170g/6 oz margarine   18p
340g/¾ lb self-raising flour   20p
A little cold water or milk

Method
1 Rub the fat into the flour until the mixture resembles fine
   breadcrumbs. Add a little water or milk and knead to a dough.
2 Divide into 2 pieces and roll the larger half for a pie-case and
   use the remainder for a lid.

Approximate cost: 38p

Dumplings

Ingredients	*Approximately*
55g/2 oz margarine	6p
115/g 4 oz self-raising wholemeal flour	7p
Salt and freshly ground black pepper	
A little water	

Method
1 Mix the margarine and the flour, then add just enough water to
   form a stiffish dough.
2 Form into pattie shapes and place on top of soup or casserole
   (arranged around the edge as dumplings in the middle take
   longer to cook) and cook for 10–12 minutes until swollen.
   (Alternatively boil in salted water 10–12 minutes.)
3 Serve immediately as dumplings left immersed too long
   become heavy.

Approximate cost of dumplings: 13p

Chapatis or Quick Bread

Ingredients	*Approximately*
170–225g/6–8 oz self-raising wholemeal flour	14p
Salt	
A little water	
Vegetable oil (6 tablespoons approximately)	5p

Method
1 Form a dough with the water and flour and salt.
2 Form into 6–8 pattie shapes and roll out thinly on a floured surface.
3 Fry in a little oil on both sides till golden and crispy. Keep warm in oven until the rest are cooked.
4 Ideal with curries and stew.

Variation:
By adding a few raisins and a little sugar, a quick raisin bread can be made.

Approximate cost of Chapatis or Quick Bread: 19p

Sauces

The basic white sauce in this book is made with wholemeal flour and has a lovely grainy texture which some may find a little unusual. Also, it is made without a roux and is, therefore, less fattening than most other white sauces.

Thin White Sauce

(For cream soups, etc.)

Ingredients	*Approximately*
850ml/1½ pints milk	39p
55g/2 oz wholemeal flour	2p

Method
1   Mix 250ml/9 fl oz of milk with the flour into a smooth paste. Stir in a further 250ml/9 fl oz of milk and bring the mixture slowly to the boil over a moderate heat, stirring constantly.
2   Gradually add the rest of the milk, stir and simmer the sauce gently for a further 10 minutes.

Approximate cost of ingredients: 41p

Medium White Sauce

This sauce is used in the Vegetable pies (pages 81, 82 and 98), Fish Pie II (page 91) and the Savoury Pancake fillings (pages 60–62).

Ingredients   *Approximately*
30ml/2 heaped tablespoons wholemeal flour per 285ml/$\frac{1}{2}$ pint milk.

Method
1   Gradually mix the flour with the milk into a smooth paste.
2   Bring the mixture to the boil, stirring all the while.
3   Cook for a further 10–15 minutes on a low heat, stirring constantly.

Cheese Sauce

Ingredients	Approximately
570ml/1 pint medium white sauce	30p
115g/4 oz Cheddar, grated	35p

Method

1 When sauce is made, add cheese and stir until thoroughly blended.

Approximate cost of ingredients: 65p

Parsley Sauce

Ingredients	Approximately
570ml/1 pint medium white sauce	30p
30ml/2 level tablespoons finely chopped fresh parsley	

Method

1 Stir the parsley into the sauce immediately before serving, in order that the parsley may remain very green and retain all its flavour.
2 When serving parsley sauce with fish, 5–10ml/1–2 teaspoons of vinegar may be added to give a piquant flavour.

Approximate cost of ingredients: 30p

Tomato Sauce

Ingredients	Approximately
2 onions, finely chopped	16p
15ml/1 tablespoon vegetable oil	
1 clove garlic, crushed	
2.5ml/½ teaspoon mixed herbs	
395g/14 oz tin tomatoes	20p
Salt	
Freshly ground black pepper	

Method
1 Gently sauté the onions in oil with garlic and herbs.
2 Heat the tomatoes in a separate saucepan, crushing them with a wooden spoon.
3 Add the sautéed onion mixture, season, cover and simmer gently 30 – 45 minutes.
4 Goes well with Rice and Mince (page 103).

Approximate cost of ingredients: 36p

Simple Salad

Although there are a selection of salads available among the recipes for dinners in the Benefit Book (some of them, a meal in themselves), the Simple Salad is here among the Basic Essentials because it is just that, basically essential to almost all my main meals, eaten with virtually all of them and recommended with nearly every dinner recipe.

Most of the ingredients for a week's worth of Simple Salads can be bought in one visit to the greengrocer. That is usually my routine, leaving only the watercress to be bought daily, owing to its tendency to become limp rather quickly if kept overnight in the refrigerator.

Of course, the ingredients listed for a Simple Salad are those I generally use, but should you find yourself short of any of them or with any other vegetables, then vary the combination. The fact is that just about any vegetable eaten cooked can also be eaten raw. So don't let that apple shrivel up, slice it into a salad; don't fry

---

- In the winter cooked vegetables such as diced potatoes, carrots, beans, cauliflower and beetroot can be used in salad.

---

all the leeks, chop some into the salad. The only essential ingredient to a Simple Salad is a most elementary oil and vinegar dressing, added five minutes before serving.

If salads aren't already a daily feature of your diet, they should be. You may feel you have to push yourself initially, but it's worth the pushing. Preparation of daily Simple Salad will soon become a 10 minute affair, and much to your benefit!

Simple Salad

Ingredients	*Approximately*
A good helping of lettuce (maybe ½ small round)	15p
½ bunch watercress	15p
1 tomato, sliced	6p
Piece cucumber, sliced	5p
1 carrot, grated	5p

Dressing:
5ml/1 teaspoon salt
Freshly ground black pepper
15ml/1 tablespoon vinegar, to taste
8ml/½ tablespoon oil, to taste

Method
1 Rinse and drain the lettuce and watercress or simply give them a good shake after rinsing. Chop them and place them in the salad bowl then add the other salad ingredients (which should also have been rinsed).

2   Mix the dressing ingredients together and add to the salad just
    before serving. Toss lightly.

Approximate cost of ingredients: 46p

Yogurt

Basically yogurt is not essential, and when on a budget of £28 per
week yogurt is essentially expensive, that is if bought by the
carton as most yogurt is. But yogurt is included in the Basic
Essentials because it is highly nutritious, low in fat and calories
and easy to make. Throughout my time in receipt of Benefit I was
also issued with 2 milk tokens per week. These made me eligible
for 14 pints of milk, hence if a milk glut was to be avoided and the
former luxury yogurt enjoyed, making my own was the solu-
tion. Furthermore, yogurt is very adaptable and can be used in
both sweet and savoury dishes, is an excellent and convenient
starter for babies and is easy to digest. Indeed, any member of a
household can benefit greatly by consuming more yogurt.

Unfortunately, store-bought varieties can prove to be expensive, and the highly flavoured pots available can be quite adulte-
rated with additives. I find it simple and economical to make my
own. You don't have to own a farm house to make yogurt, it's
really quite convenient once you know how and positively indul-
gent creating your own wholesome flavours. Those over-ripe
strawberries you bought cheaply make an excellent addition:
yogurt drinks are delicious and can be thinned down with water or
fruit juice and yogurt dressings and dips are very appetizing. In
fact, yogurt is extremely versatile.

It is not necessary to have a yogurt maker, but some find that
using one makes the process easier. I use just an ordinary
enamelled, cast-iron casserole with a lid, and it does the job well
enough for me. A heavy glass casserole or earthenware pot with
lid can be used equally successfully and incubated in a *warm* (not
hot) oven, a warm airing cupboard or simply near a hot radiator.
Alternatively, a thermos flask can be used.

Non-fat Dry-milk Yogurt

(Makes 850ml/1½ pints of yogurt)
Ingredients

115g/4 oz non-fat dry-milk powder (or more if a richer concentra-
    tion is desired)
720ml/1¼ pints hot water
60ml/2 fl oz plain yogurt (commercial or home-made)

Method
1   Beat or blend milk powder with hot water until all the granules
    are dissolved (an electric blender is fine at this stage). Then
    pour the mixture into the container and beat the yogurt in
    lightly (being careful to ensure that the mixture is not too hot
    and is around 55°C/110°F).
2   Cover and incubate. It is important to *remember not to move*
    the container during this period or the yogurt will separate. The
    yogurt should set within 3½ hours. If after that time it hasn't,
    repeat the process and use a fresh commercial starter.

Fresh Milk Yogurt

All milk must first be scalded (brought almost to the boil) to kill off
any bacteria that might prevent the growth of yogurt culture. The
milk must next be left to cool down until it is hand-hot (55°C/
110°F).

● To scald food or milk: pour boiling water over food
  and let stand for a few minutes. To scald milk is to
  bring it almost to the boil.

Ingredients
1.1 litres/2 pints milk (skimmed or whole)
55g/2 oz dry milk powder
60ml/2 fl oz unflavoured yogurt (commercial or home-made)

Method
1 Scald the milk then add the milk powder whilst the milk is still very hot. If desired, the mixture can be made smoother by pouring through a fine strainer and forcing through with a small wooden spoon.
2 Leave to cool for approximately 15 minutes then add a little milk to the yogurt and beat lightly with a fork.
3 Add this to the rest of the milk and beat briefly. Incubate as outlined above. (Makes 1.1 litres/2 pints.)

Frying Pan with Lid

The reason for inclusion of this one most inedible item among the Basic Essentials is that the method of cooking most frequently employed when preparing the many dishes in the Benefit Book is to sauté (fry lightly in a little oil). Covering the frying pan with a lid will help retain both heat and moisture, reduce frying time, make the kitchen less hot and steamy and ensure the foods cooked retain maximum flavour.

Sadly, good cast-iron frying pans with lids can prove difficult to find and as my own orange enamelled pan-set did not include one, I improvised and successfully used the slightly narrower lid of the casserole dish, in a slightly sunken position to cover all my fast-frying-meals.

Care of your cast-iron pan
It is important after using a frying pan for meat and certain other dishes, apart from merely sautéing vegetables, to wash and rinse it out thoroughly. After that it helps to wipe it with a clean cloth then dry it over a low heat. Add 15ml/1 tablespoon of oil and tilt pan so that the oil spreads around. This prevents the pan from rusting.

Hints — Tips — and Suggestions

On buying vegetables

When buying vegetables see that the green ones are not yellow but a fresh green colour and crisp. Root vegetables should be firm and not coarse. Tomatoes should be firm and red but if bought a little green can be ripened in a dark drawer. Potatoes should be firm and have no shoots. Lettuce and other salad vegetables should be crisp.

On boiling vegetables

Most vegetables should be cooked in a small amount of water and covered while cooking. When cooking frozen peas add 15ml/1 tablespoon water, 1 knob of margarine or butter and a little salt. Double the amount of water when cooking fresh peas. Cover the peas (455g/1 lb frozen) and cook on a very low light, stirring occasionally, for about 10–15 minutes. Greens can be shredded and cooked by the 455g/1 lb with 60ml/4 tablespoons water, a knob of margarine or butter and salt. Cook until tender but not soggy. Spinach should not be shredded but covered and cooked with a drop of water and a knob of margarine and seasoned to taste. Cook on a low heat for about 5 minutes. Once the vegetables are cooked, strain them and save the liquid for stocks and soups.

2
Breakfasts

Breakfast time in most households tends to be a rather rushed part of the day. Even in a home where the breadwinner has been effectively grounded with no workplace to get to, if there are youngsters either hurrying out to, or to be taken out to school, then the pressure (to get them washed, dressed, fed and out) remains on at breakfast time.

This, the rushed nature of breakfast time, must be a major factor in the monumental success over the years of the numerous so-called 'breakfast cereals' available on the shelves of every supermarket. Preparation of these 'breakfasts' is merely a matter of pouring them into a bowl, covering them with milk and (if not already caked in sugar coating) showering them with sugar (though I did once know a boy who put sugar even on sugared cereal), to be then gobbled down most enthusiastically in minutes by non-complaining youngsters.

Many such products boast graphs or lists of their mineral or vitamin content, placed strategically upon the sides of their boxes to dazzle and impress their consumer whilst wolfing them down at the table. But all too often these are artificially produced vitamins added to an otherwise relatively deficient product and, even in the cases of the few such breakfast cereals where the product is quite fibrous and without additives, one pays dearly for the little one gets. (I do recall reading many years ago in a national daily of an outbreak of mice in a factory producing a leading breakfast cereal. The result of this was extensive rodential damage to the outer cardboard boxes, the costly contents of which went untouched. Anything mice have the sense to leave alone can't be too nourishing!)

I myself have long regarded all boxed cereals containing artificial flavouring, colouring or preservatives, as many do, most unsuitable for a good breakfast and, luckily, I never did start any of my kids on breakfast cereals. Artificial colouring is (in my books) particularly important to avoid because it is being increasingly recognized as a factor in hyperactivity among sensitive children and is also an often unsuspected cause of much discomfort and suffering when it triggers allergies of which many of us are wholly unaware.

Finally, all such cereals rely heavily upon the milk in which they are soaked to nourish their consumer as they lack any of their own natural staying power, hence we have seen the advent of elevenses — when many of those reliant upon such breakfasts are seen ravenously eating snacks of sorts — usually further produce of the junk food giants.

Thus the truth of the matter is that should you or members of your household have been reliant upon such products for some time, then both you and the kids would be better off, in terms of nourishment as well as cash in the pocket, simply by serving yourselves a bowl of oats with a few raisins added (Miser's Muesli) or sitting down to a bowl of hot and hearty porridge for your breakfasts.

Of course, initially, least enthusiastic to give up their morning meals of mass produced breakfast cereals may be the children. But when it comes to the crunch I do urge you to persevere because kids, not so set in their ways, are quite flexible and can quickly adapt themselves to changes, unlike most of us adults, and if your kids understand that their newly adopted set of meals is not only going to be better for them in terms of health, but is also going to enable you to give them more pocket money or funding for that long sought garment or special activity, their co-operation should be achieved without too much difficulty.

So here are some 13 suggestions for breakfasts. All are eaten

---

● Separate the £28 shopping budget from all your other money: this way you can see visibly when you are invading your other monies.

in this household, though some are naturally more occasional than others: Simple Bread Cereal, for instance, is usually a last resort. Several of these preparations were a craze for some time — that is literally the only breakfast eaten day after day, for weeks on end. But the one single food eaten most frequently by ourselves for breakfast over the years must be toast — good old wholemeal toast, that is. When it comes to spreads, or toppings, each member of our household seems to have a particular preference: maybe peanut butter or yeast extract or marmalade, but nobody ever seems to tire of good old wholemeal toast, day in day out, year after year, toast is a favourite for their breakfast.

Oat Porridge

(Serves 4–6)

Ingredients	*Approximately*
115g/4 oz porridge oats	8p
850ml–1.1 litres/1½–2 pints milk (whole, skimmed or re-constituted)	42p

Method
1 Bring oats and milk to the boil, stirring occasionally. Simmer 2–5 minutes, stirring all the time.
2 Serve with brown sugar or honey. Nut, seed or soy milks may also be used.

Approximate cost: 50p

Miser's Muesli

(1 serving)

Ingredients	*Approximately*
55g/2 oz porridge oats	4p
15–30ml/1–2 tablespoons seedless raisins or sultanas	7p
150ml/5 fl oz milk (whole, skimmed or soy etc.)	7p

Method
1 Mix oatmeal with the dried fruit. Sprinkle with brown sugar or honey if desired. (To reduce the amount of sweetening needed, add 2.5ml/½ teaspoon vanilla extract to each 240ml/ 8 fl oz of milk.)
2 Top with milk or yogurt sweetened with honey (30ml/2 table-spoons yogurt — 5ml/1 teaspoon honey).
3 Can also be served with sliced banana, peaches or any berry in season.

Approximate cost: 18p

Cornmeal Porridge

(4–6 servings)

Ingredients	*Approximately*
140g/5 oz cornmeal (fine)	7p
1.1–1.7 litres/2–2½ pints milk (whole, re-constituted or soy etc.)	66p

Method
1 Stir cornmeal with the milk. Bring to the boil, cook 10 minutes stirring often.
2 Sweeten with brown sugar or honey. Serve hot.

Approximate cost: 73p

Cornmeal Pudding

(4–6 servings)

Ingredients	*Approximately*
140g/5 oz cornmeal (fine)	7p
850ml–1.1 litres/1½–2 pints milk	42p

Method
1 Stir the cornmeal into the milk. Bring to the boil and cook for 10 minutes, stirring often.
2 Serve the hot thick cornmeal with butter or cottage cheese and salt or jam.

Approximate cost: 49p

Toast Cereal

(Serves 4)

Ingredients	*Approximately*
6 slices wholemeal bread	12p
15ml/1 tablespoon honey or brown sugar	5p
570ml/1 pint milk	26p

Method
1 Toast, lightly butter and dice the bread. Divide into serving bowls.
2 Sweeten the milk with honey or sugar. Heat, then pour over the toast cubes.

Approximate cost: 43p

Bread Cereal

(Serves 4)

Ingredients	*Approximately*
6 slices wholemeal bread	12p
90ml/6 tablespoons seedless raisins or sultanas	21p
570ml/1 pint milk	26p

Method
1 Dice and divide bread into serving bowls.
2 Sprinkle with raisins and, if desired, brown sugar.
3 Heat milk and pour onto bread cubes.

Approximate cost: 59p

Simple Bread Cereal

Use crusts from trimmed bread or stale bread and chop coarsely.
Let stand uncovered overnight to dry. Store in airtight container.
Serve as cereal with dried fruit.

Grilled Banana

(1 serving)

Ingredients	*Approximately*
1 medium banana	15p

Method
1 Make a slit in banana skin from end to end. Grill under a
moderate heat for 10 minutes.

2 Serve in peel with jam and yogurt inserted in the slit.

Approximate cost: 15p

Popcorn Surprise

(Serves 4)

Ingredients	*Approximately*
45ml/3 tablespoons vegetable oil	
45ml/3 tablespoons popcorn	15p
850ml/1$\frac{1}{2}$ pints milk	39p

Method
1 Heat the oil in a pan with a tight fitting lid (a large pan or pressure cooker is ideal for this). Add popcorn and cover. The corn will start to pop as it cooks over a moderate heat.
2 When the popping sounds cease the popcorn is ready.
3 Sweeten to taste with brown sugar and add milk.

Approximate cost: 54p

Eggs — Basic Methods of Cooking

Softboiled
Lower gently into boiling water and simmer gently for 3 minutes. If put into cold water, bring gently to the boil and simmer gently for 2$\frac{1}{2}$–3 minutes. After the eggs have cooked plunge them into cold water to prevent them cooking further with their own heat. Eggs taken from the refrigerator often require an extra $\frac{1}{2}$–1 minute cooking and the cold water method is best. 5ml/1 level teaspoon of salt in the cooking water will help to prevent the shells cracking. If the shells crack, 5ml/1 teaspoon of vinegar will help to prevent the egg white from dispersing in the water.

Hard-boiled
Gently simmer eggs for 15 minutes. Eggs lowered into boiling water are more likely to have their yolks in the centre than those

put into cold water. To avoid a dark ring around the yolk, do not over-boil, and do plunge the eggs after cooking into cold water.

Coddled
Place eggs in their shells in a pan of boiling water. Cover and remove pan from heat. Leave for 10 minutes, then serve.

Poached
Have ready a shallow pan containing lightly-salted water. Break eggs, one at a time, into a cup or saucer and slip gently into the simmering water. Cover and remove pan from heat, and leave in a warm place until whites have set and a thin film has formed over the yolks. Lift them out with a perforated spoon, and serve on buttered toast. If an egg poacher is used, butter shells before breaking an egg into each. Cover and steam until set.

Scrambled Eggs

Ingredients	*Approximately*
4 eggs	32p
Salt and freshly ground black pepper	
30ml/2 tablespoons milk	
30g/1 oz margarine or butter	3p

Method
1 Beat the eggs with seasoning and milk.
2 Melt the margarine or butter in a small saucepan, pour in the egg mixture and stir over a moderate heat until the mixture has set creamily but is still moist.
3 Alternatively, melt the fat (or use vegetable oil) then beat the eggs, seasoning and milk in the pan with a wooden spoon. Cook as before.

Approximate cost of ingredients: 35p

3
Lunches

Almost all the recipes for lunches in the Benefit Book are substantial enough to serve as a main meal or as the main part of a dinner. All, that is, with the exception of sweet pancakes, perhaps. Thus, it is no strange thing in this household to sit down at dinner-time to Cream of Mackerel Soup served with a heap of bread buns and garnished with watercress, or Savoury pancakes with baked potatoes and salad.

But, after having baked bread earlier in the morning but not having yet gone out to the shops, it is often very convenient to use up the few vegetables remaining in the cupboard or remnants (of either fish or meat) from last night's dinner in a soup, most convenient. Hence, it is usually in the last hour of the morning that I find myself preparing soups, soups to be consumed for lunch. Likewise, the ingredients for a Savoury Pancake filling such as Sweet Corn and Mushrooms or Cream Cheese and Spinach will often be available to use up, and when wrapped in a pancake they become great favourites with the kids.

Now, upon reading some of the recipes for soups, the initial thought of making a sauce while sautéing vegetables, before mixing and seasoning them, may seem rather a lot of needless labour to many non-cooks when one can simply open a tin, warm the contents and — abracadabra — lunch (a soup) is ready. But there is no comparison in either quality or cost. You're best off in both respects making your own meals, real meals. In my earliest days rendered jobless, it was the newly discovered activity of preparing quality meals which proved a great alternative to those idle hours of twiddling thumbs, which is when the erosion of one's morale can otherwise set in.

However, having said all that, I must confess that in my opinion nothing beats bread as a base for lunches. I never tire of it, nor will you if you're making the real stuff! The choice is endless, toasted or not, anything from smoked salmon sandwiches to banana butties, pâtés, cooked meats, cheeses and vegetable spreads. For quickness, ease and convenience, in my opinion, at lunch-time, 'nowt beats butties!'

Welsh Rarebit

(Serves 2–3)

Ingredients	*Approximately*
115g/4 oz grated cheese	35p
45ml/3 tablespoon milk	4p
Salt and freshly ground black pepper	
15ml/1 tablespoon margarine or butter	2p
4–6 slices toast	12p

Method
1 Place the cheese and milk in a saucepan and melt slowly.
2 Add the pepper, salt and margarine or butter.
3 When hot, pour over the toast and brown under the grill until bubbling. (Sometimes a little beer is added to the mixture.)

Approximate cost of ingredients: 53p

Sardines on Toast

Ingredients	*Approximately*
120g/4¼ oz tin sardines	29p
55g/2 oz grated cheese	18p
15ml/1 tablespoon margarine or butter	2p
Salt and freshly ground black pepper	
15ml/1 tablespoon milk or yogurt	2p
4–6 slices toast	12p

Method

1 Mash the sardines and combine with most of the cheese and the other ingredients.
2 Pile the mixture on the toast. Sprinkle with the remaining cheese and brown under the grill.

Approximate cost of ingredients: 60p

Sandwich suggestions (priced and unpriced)

Taramasalata and salad on wholemeal bread (12 slices) 79p.
Humous spread and salad on wholemeal bread (12 slices) 73p.
Mackerel pâté and salad on wholemeal bread (12 slices) 89p.
Ham and salad on wholemeal bread (12 slices) £1.39.
Crab pâté and salad on wholemeal bread (12 slices) £1.04.
Chicken and salad on wholemeal bread.
Tuna fish and sweetcorn on wholemeal bread.
Smoked mackerel mashed with yogurt garnished with thinly sliced orange.
Tinned sardines (pilchards) mashed with yogurt or salad cream and black pepper.
Cottage cheese and olives on wholemeal bread.
Cold cooked beans mashed with yeast extract, herbs and garnished with salad.
Yeast extract, cheese and salad on wholemeal bread.
Hard-boiled eggs and grated cheese mashed with salad cream or yogurt with black pepper.
Hard-boiled eggs and salad with salad cream or yogurt dressing.
Scrambled egg on its own or with sweetcorn or mushroom.
Toasted cheese sandwich (12 slices) with salad 94p.
Baked beans on toast (8 slices) 74p.

- Cutting fresh new bread can prove difficult if still warm. Hence, if unable to wait for bread to cool stand the knife in boiling water for a few minutes first.

Omelettes – Basic Method

If possible keep a special pan for omelette making, and wipe out with paper after use to preserve an oily surface. For a 3–4 egg omelette you will need a pan about 23cm/9 inches in diameter, and for a 6 egg omelette, the pan should be about 25cm/10 inches in diameter.

Eggs for omelettes should not be beaten too much: 30 seconds' beating with a fork is sufficient. Do not let the butter in the pan brown or the omelette may stick. Never mix milk with eggs for omelettes as it will make them tough.

Chinese Omelette

Ingredients	Approximately
4 eggs	32p
60ml/4 tablespoon water	
Salt and freshly ground black pepper	
4 onions, finely chopped	15p
55g/2 oz beansprouts	15p
30ml/2 tablespoons vegetable oil	
225g/½ lb cooked lean pork or chicken, diced	75p

Method
1 Lightly beat the eggs. Add water and seasoning and whisk together.
2 In a pan other than the one to be used for the omelette, sauté the onion and beansprouts in a little oil. Add the cooked meat and continue to stir-fry until the onion is tender and the mixture piping hot.
3 Heat the omelette pan, add a little oil and when hot, add half the egg mixture. When the bottom of the egg mixture has set, spoon over a layer of meat mixture.
4 Cover with more of the egg and continue to cook like an omelette, shaking the pan occasionally until the mixture has almost set. Turn over and brown the other side.
5 Suitable for lunch or for dinner with hot rice and soya sauce.

Approximate cost of ingredients: £1.37

Yorkshire Omelette

Ingredients	Approximately
4 potatoes, cooked	20p
115g/4 oz bacon	25p
30ml/2 tablespoons vegetable oil	
5 eggs	40p
2.5ml/$\frac{1}{2}$ teaspoon mixed herbs	
Salt and freshly ground black pepper	

Method

1 Cut the potatoes and bacon into small pieces and fry the bacon first and then the potatoes, in the vegetable oil.
2 Beat the eggs, add the bacon, potatoes, herbs and seasoning.
3 Cook until the mixture has almost set then turn and brown the other side. Serve flat.

Approximate cost of ingredients: 85p

Cheese Omelette

Ingredients	Approximately
6 eggs	50p
15ml/1 tablespoon cold water	
Salt and freshly ground black pepper	
30g/1 oz butter or margarine	3p
55g/2 oz grated cheese	21p

Method
1 Beat the eggs and water with a fork for 30 seconds. Add seasoning.
2 Melt the butter in an omelette pan and when it is sizzling hot but not brown, add the eggs.
3 Sprinkle over the cheese and cook over a moderate heat, lifting the edges so that the uncooked part can run underneath. When it is firm but still soft on top it is ready.
4 Fold the omelette over the cheese and serve either with wholemeal bread at lunchtime or with baked potatoes and salad at dinner time.

Approximate cost of ingredients: 74p

Ham Omelette

Ingredients	Approximately
1 onion, chopped	8p
15ml/1 tablespoon vegetable oil	
115g/4 oz cooked ham, diced	55p
6 eggs	50p

Method
1 Sauté the onion until soft, add the ham and continue cooking for 1–2 minutes. Pour on the beaten eggs.
2 Stir once or twice with a fork and lift the edges so that the uncooked part can run underneath.

3   When set, fold over and serve either at lunch or dinner time.

Approximate cost of ingredients: £1.13

Mushroom Omelette

Ingredients	*Approximately*
115g/4 oz mushrooms, chopped	30p
15ml/1 tablespoon vegetable oil	
5ml/ 1 teaspoon lemon juice	
Salt and freshly ground black pepper	
6 eggs	50p

Method
1   Sauté the mushrooms in the oil, lemon juice and seasoning for 30 seconds then cover and cook over a gentle heat for 5 minutes.
2   Meanwhile, beat the eggs with 15ml/1 tablespoon of water and seasoning and use this mixture to make an omelette.
3   When it has set, fill with the mushrooms mixture, fold over and serve immediately.

Approximate cost of ingredients: 80p

Pancakes
Savoury Pancakes

Ingredients	Approximately
225g/½ lb wholemeal flour	9p
A good pinch salt	
5ml/1 level teaspoon baking powder	
1 egg	8p
570ml/ 1 pint milk	26p
Vegetable oil	

Method
1 Thoroughly mix the flour, salt and baking powder. Make a well in the centre and break in the egg. Add the milk slowly, beating until the mixture is smooth. Leave to stand for 30 minutes. Or, mix the batter in a blender starting with the milk and egg and gradually adding the flour.
2 Heat a little oil in a frying pan (preferably cast iron) and pour in 30ml/2 tablespoon of batter. Tilt the pan so that the batter spreads evenly. Cook over a moderate heat until bubbles form on the surface. Slide a spatula under the pancake and flip it over to cook the second side.
3 Keep the pancakes hot in the oven until ready for filling.

Approximate cost of ingredients: 43p

Chicken or Fish and Mushroom Pancake Filling

Ingredients	Approximately
¼ cooked chicken or 455g/1 lb fish fillets	90p
285ml/½ pint medium white sauce	14p
55g/2 oz mushrooms, sautéed	15p
Salt and freshly ground black pepper	

Method

1 Shred the chicken or flake the cooked fish and mix with the sauce. Add the cooked mushrooms and season to taste.
2 Fill each pancake with 15ml/1 tablespoon of the mixture and roll each one up.
3 Lay them side by side in a greased baking dish and cook in a moderate oven at 180°C/350°F (Gas Mark 4) for about 15 minutes.

Approximate cost of ingredients: £1.59

Mushroom, Onion and Beansprout Pancake Filling

Ingredients	*Approximately*
55g/2 oz mushrooms, sliced	15p
1 onion, sliced	8p
115g/4 oz beansprouts, chopped	20p
15–30ml/1–2 tablespoons vegetable oil	
15ml/1 tablespoon soya sauce	

Method

1 Sauté the vegetables in a little oil for 10 minutes.
2 Add the soya sauce and use to fill pancakes.

Approximate cost of ingredients for 4 savoury pancakes: 83p

Sweetcorn and Mushroom Pancake Filling

Ingredients	*Approximately*
1 onion, sliced	8p
55g/2 oz mushrooms, sliced	15p
115g/4 oz fresh sweetcorn kernels (or frozen)	15p
15–30ml/1–2 tablespoons vegetable oil	
285ml/$\frac{1}{2}$ pint medium white sauce	14p

Method
1 Sauté the vegetables in a little oil for 10–15 minutes.
2 Add the white sauce, season and use to fill pancakes.

Approximate cost of ingredients for 4 savoury pancakes: 92p

Cream Cheese and Spinach Pancake Filling

Ingredients	*Approximately*
1 onion, sliced	8p
15ml/1 tablespoon vegetable oil	
225g/$\frac{1}{2}$ lb spinach, washed and chopped	36p
115g/4 oz cream cheese	40p

Method
1 Sauté the onion in oil for 5 minutes. Add the spinach and sauté for a further 5–10 minutes.
2 Take off the heat and stir in the cream cheese. Use to fill the pancakes.

Approximate cost of ingredients for 4 savoury pancakes: £1.24

Pancakes (Sweet)

Ingredients	Approximately
4 eggs	32p
285ml/½ pint milk	13p
115g/4 oz wholemeal flour	4p
100–150ml/6–7 tablespoons vegetable oil	
Honey and lemon	
Fruit of choice	30p

Method

1 Add the eggs and milk gradually to the flour and beat well to make a smooth batter. Alternatively, mix the batter in a blender starting with the eggs and milk and gradually adding the flour.
2 If possible let the batter stand in the refrigerator for 30 minutes or more.
3 Transfer the batter to a jug and pour 30ml/2 tablespoons at a time into a hot, heavy based frying pan greased with 10–15ml/ 2–3 teaspoons oil. Tilt the pan so that the batter spreads.
4 Cook over a moderate heat and when bubbles form on the surface, slide a spatula under the pancake and flip it over to cook the other side.
5 Keep the pancakes hot in the oven until ready to fill.
6 To serve, spread each pancake with honey and lemon and fill with sliced banana or peaches or strawberries or ice cream or a mixture. Roll them up and serve with yogurt if liked.

Approximate cost of ingredients for 4 pancakes: 86p

Soups

Tomato Bouillon

Ingredients	*Approximately*
300g/11 oz jar tomato purée	49p
850ml/1½ pints stock (or water with 15ml/1 tablespoon yeast extract)	15p
5ml/1 teaspoon brown sugar	
Salt and freshly ground black pepper	
Finely chopped parsley	

Method
1 Bring the tomato purée and stock to the boil. Add the sugar and seasoning to taste.
2 Sprinkle with chopped parsley and serve with toast.

Approximate cost of ingredients: 64p

Mulligatawny Soup

Ingredients	*Approximately*
300g/11 oz split red lentils	33p
850ml–1 litre/1½–2 pints stock (or water with 15ml/1 tablespoon yeast extract)	5p
15ml/1 tablespoon curry powder	15p
15ml/1 tablespoon vegetable oil	
2 carrots, grated	10p
2 onions, sliced	16p
1 apple, cored and chopped	10p
Crushed garlic to taste	10p
Salt	
Juice ½ lemon	5p

Method
1 Bring the lentils to the boil in the stock with the curry powder.

Spiced pork and beans

Lentil flan, quick quiche and green salad

Spiced mackerel and stir-fry vegetables

Vegetable curry and brown rice

Macaroni chicken and simple salad

Blackeye beanburgers with baked potato

Miser's muesli and cornmeal pudding with jam

Tomato bouillon, cream of mackerel soup and bargain bread

2   Meanwhile, heat the oil and sauté the carrots, onions, apple and garlic for 15 minutes.
3   Add the vegetables to the stock and simmer for 30 minutes. Season and stir in lemon juice.

Approximate cost of ingredients: £1.04

Minestrone Soup

Ingredients	Approximately
55g/2 oz wholewheat spaghetti, broken into small pieces	5p
850ml–1 litre/1½–2 pints stock (or water with 15ml/ 1 tablespoon yeast extract)	15p
55g/2 oz chopped bacon, optional	12p
115g/4 oz porridge oats	8p
115g/4 oz cabbage, finely chopped	12p
1 turnip, grated	5p
1 onion, sliced	8p
Oil, as necessary	
Salt and freshly ground black pepper	
Pinch dried or freshly chopped thyme	

Method
1   Bring the spaghetti to the boil in the stock.
2   Sauté the bacon, oats and vegetables with a little oil if necessary, for 15 minutes. Add them to the soup stock and simmer for 30 minutes. Season to taste.

Approximate cost of ingredients: 60p

- A ham bone, or bits of left-over ham and bacon make a good stock and go especially well with lentils.

Lentil Soup

Ingredients   *Approximately*
300g/11 oz red split lentils   34p
1.1 litres/2 pints water
3 carrots, grated   15p
2 onions, sliced   10p
Crushed garlic, to taste   16p
1 medium leek, chopped   25p
15ml/1 tablespoon vegetable oil (soya etc.)
15ml/ 1 tablespoon soya sauce
7.5ml/$\frac{1}{2}$ tablespoon tomato purée
Salt and freshly ground black pepper

Method
1 Bring the lentils to the boil in the water.
2 Sauté the vegetables in oil for 15 minutes and add to soup stock. Add the soya sauce and tomato purée. Season and simmer for 25 minutes.
3 Serve with wholemeal bread or dumplings.

Approximate cost of Lentil Soup: £1.00

Cream of Mackerel Soup

Ingredients	*Approximately*
1 carrot, grated	5p
1 onion, sliced	8p
Crushed garlic, to taste	10p
15ml/1 tablespoon vegetable oil	
1 small mackerel, filleted	50p
55g/2 oz mushrooms, sliced	15p
30ml/2 tablespoons finely chopped parsley	5p
55g/2 oz wholemeal flour	5p
850ml–l litre/1$\frac{1}{2}$–2 pints milk (or milk and water)	46p
Salt and freshly ground black pepper	

Method

1 Sauté the carrot, onion and garlic in oil for 10 minutes. Add the fish, cover and cook for a further 10 minutes. Add the mushrooms and parsley.
2 Meanwhile, make a white sauce using the Basic White Sauce method (page 36). Simmer the sauce gently for 5–10 minutes stirring often and thin down if liked with more milk or water (about 285ml/$\frac{1}{2}$ pint).
3 Add the cooked vegetables and fish, stir well and season. The fish should flake nicely and the soup turn golden.

Approximate cost of ingredients: £1.44

Cream of Chicken Soup

Ingredients   *Approximately*
1 small piece chicken   65p
15ml/1 tablespoon vegetable oil
2 stalks celery, chopped   10p
1 onion, sliced   8p
55g/2 oz frozen peas   4p
55g/2 oz wholemeal flour   5p
850ml–l litre/1½–2 pints milk (or milk and water)   46p
Salt and freshly ground black pepper

Method
1   If not using cooked chicken, sauté the chicken in the oil for 15
    minutes in a covered pan then add the vegetables, stir, cover
    and sauté for a further 10–15 minutes.
2   Meanwhile, make a white sauce using the Basic White Sauce
    method (page 36).
3   Bone and shred the chicken and add it to the white sauce with
    the vegetables. Stir, season and serve with bread dough
    dumplings or bargain bread.

Approximate cost of ingredients: £1.38

Variation:

Boxing Day Soup

Follow the Cream of Chicken Soup recipe substituting turkey for
the chicken.

Cream of Mushroom Soup

Ingredients	*Approximately*
1 carrot, grated	5p
1 onion, sliced	8p
115g/4 oz mushrooms, chopped	30p
15ml/1 tablespoon vegetable oil	
55g/2 oz wholemeal flour	5p
850ml–l litre/1½–2 pints milk	46p
Salt and freshly ground black pepper	

Method

1 Sauté the carrot, onion and mushrooms in the vegetable oil for about 15 minutes.
2 Meanwhile make a white sauce from the flour and milk using the Basic White Sauce method (page 36).
3 Add the vegetables, season and cook for a further 10–15 minutes, stirring occasionally.
4 Serve with wholemeal bread or dumplings.

Approximate cost of ingredients: 94p

Cream of Celery Soup

Ingredients	*Approximately*
6 celery stalks, diced	30p
1 onion, sliced	8p
1 small bunch parsley, finely chopped	5p
15ml/1 tablespoon vegetable oil	
55g/2 oz wholemeal flour	5p
850ml–l litre/1½–2 pints milk (or milk and water)	46p
Salt and freshly ground black pepper	

Method

1 Sauté the celery, onion and parsley in vegetable oil for 15 minutes.
2 Make a white sauce with the flour and milk using the Basic White Sauce method (page 36).
3 Add the vegetables, season and cook for a further 10–15 minutes. Serve with wholemeal bread or dumplings.

Approximate cost of ingredients: 94p

Spring Vegetable Soup

Ingredients	*Approximately*
115g/4 oz fresh or frozen peas	8p
1 stick celery, chopped	5p
1 young carrot, grated	5p
1 medium onion, sliced	8p
55g/2 oz mushrooms, chopped	15p
15ml/1 tablespoon vegetable oil	
55g/2 oz wholemeal flour	
850ml–1 litre/1½–2 pints milk (or milk and water)	46p
Salt and freshly ground black pepper	

Method
1 Sauté the vegetables in the oil for about 15 minutes.
2 Make a white sauce with the flour and milk using the Basic White Sauce method (page 36).
3 Add the vegetables and seasoning to the sauce. Cook for a further 10–15 minutes, stirring occasionally.

Approximate cost of ingredients: 87p

4
Main Meals

Now last, but by no means least, are the Benefit Book's dinner recipes, not all dinners in themselves but it's at dinner time that I tend to serve them. Two of these meals are weekly preparations in this kitchen: Roast Chicken and Quick Quiche. Week in, week out, nobody tires of them and there'd be some jolly stern questions from the kids to answer should I let a week pass without them. But for the remaining five nights of the week I refer to my dinner list, in order to keep our menu varied but within budget, and suggest that you do likewise.

It often helps to plan a meal in advance, for example, when making Cowboy Beans, if wishing to have dinner at 5 o'clock, it's best to put the beans on to cook at 2 o'clock. Alternatively, red kidney beans can be cooked in large batches and some frozen for future use. Those persons cooking for themselves or two people at the most can freeze the surplus or divide the ingredients in the recipes more or less in half.

If some of the recipes don't turn out quite right — don't despair, try again! Don't lose confidence, you'll soon get the hang of it. Your creation may not look nice, but if you've basically stuck by the recipe, it will be very edible! (So many of our meals today are designed to please the eye but not the belly.) Cooking is a science, a domestic science, and you mustn't be afraid to experiment — if you feel like substituting the vegetables in a recipe for some others, do so. Go ahead, have fun and, above all, relax!

On pages 122–26 there are some exemplary menus. Each is for an entire week's meals and each week's selection should be attainable within the figure of £28. Use these as an initial guide and you should soon be selecting your own combinations to suit both your taste and your pocket.

- When freezing make up large batches of burgers, rissoles, fishcakes, stews, soups, main meals, etc. Food will also keep for several days in a fridge.

Blackeye Beanburgers

(Serves 4)

Ingredients	Approximately
300g/11 oz blackeye beans	45p
850ml/30 fl oz water	
Salt and freshly ground black pepper	
2 small onions, chopped	16p
3 cloves garlic, crushed	10p
60ml/4 tablespoons vegetable oil	
170g/6 oz sage and onion stuffing	30p
Flour, for shaping	

Method
1 Boil the beans in the water for 10 minutes. Lower the heat cover and simmer for 1 hour (do not add salt until cooked). When cooked, season the beans.
2 Sauté the onions and garlic in 15ml/1 tablespoon of the oil and add them with the stuffing to the lentils. Mash with a potato masher then shape into burgers and roll them in a little flour.
3 Leave to stand on a wire rack for 10 minutes then fry in oil for about 10 minutes on each side or bake in oil at 200°C/400°F (Gas Mark 6) for 10 minutes, adding more oil if necessary. Serve with baked potatoes and salad.

Approximate cost of ingredients: £1.01

> • Try to maximize oven use i.e., cook burgers in a roasting tin and, instead of boiling potatoes, bake potatoes on the top rung of the oven at the same time.

Variation:

Redbean Burgers

(Serves 4)

Method
Substitute 300g/11 oz of red kidney beans for the blackeye beans in the recipe above simmering the red beans for 2 hours (or if they have been soaked overnight, simmer for 1½ hours, or pressure cook for 15 minutes). Continue as for blackeye burgers using the same ingredients.

Approximate cost of ingredients: £1.01

Blackeye Bean Stew with Dumplings

Ingredients	*Approximately*
455g/1 lb potatoes chopped	10p
150g/5½ oz blackeye beans	20p
1.7 litres/3 pints water	
10ml/2 teaspns yeast extract	
2 carrots, sliced	10p
4 onions, sliced	15p
Crushed garlic, to taste	10p
Piece cucumber, chopped large	15p
8ml/½ tablespoon tomato purée	
Salt and freshly ground black pepper	

Dumplings:
115g/4 oz wholemeal flour (1 cup)   7p
55g/2 oz margarine   6p
Salt and freshly ground black pepper
A little water

Method
1 Bring the potatoes and beans to the boil with the yeast extract.
   Cover and simmer.
2 Sauté the vegetables, starting with the carrots and ending with
   the cucumber, for 10–15 minutes. Combine the vegetables
   with the beans and potatoes.
3 Add the tomato purée and season with salt and pepper. Cover
   and simmer gently for 10–15 minutes.
4 Add the dumplings (see page 35 of Basic Essentials), cover and
   cook for a further 10 minutes till the dumplings swell.
   Serve immediately.

Alternatively:
Replace the blackeye beans with 300g/11 oz red split lentils. This
can be cooked in the oven as a casserole. Prepare the beans and
vegetables as before. Place in a casserole and bake at a
moderate heat for 15–20 minutes. Add the dumplings during the
last 10 minutes.

Approximate cost of ingredients: 93p

Blackeye Bean Bake

Ingredients	*Approximately*
250g/9 oz blackeye beans	35p
850ml/1½ pints water	
3 carrots, sliced	15p
3 onions, sliced	20p
Crushed garlic, to taste	10p
15–30ml/1½ tablespoons vegetable oil	
5ml/1 teaspoon yeast extract	5p
7.5ml/½ tablespoon tomato purée	
Salt and freshly ground black pepper	

Topping:

900g/2 lb boiled potatoes	20p
30g/1 oz margarine	3p
115g/4 oz grated cheese	35p

Method

1 Boil the beans in the water until they are cooked — about 30 minutes.
2 Sauté the carrots, onions and garlic in oil for about 10 minutes until soft. Add the beans and any remaining water.
3 Add the yeast extract, tomato purée and seasoning and spoon into a greased baking dish.
4 Mash the potatoes and margarine with the grated cheese. Season and spread over the bean mixture.
5 Bake at 180°C/350°F (Gas Mark 4) for 15 minutes or until piping hot. Serve with salad.

Approximate cost of ingredients: £1.43

Quick Quiche

(Serves 4)

Ingredients	*Approximately*
225g/½ lb wholemeal flour	8p
115g/4 oz margarine	12p
A little cold water, to mix	
3 medium onions, chopped	20p
30–45ml/2–3 tablespoons vegetable oil	
225g/½ lb grated Cheddar	70p
3 eggs	25p
Salt and freshly ground black pepper	

Method
1 Rub the flour and margarine together to make a breadcrumb-like mixture. Add a little cold water to form a dough and use to line a flan case. Prick all over with a fork and bake blind at 170°C/325°F (Gas Mark 3) for 10 minutes.
2 Meanwhile, sauté the onion in a little oil over a low heat for 5–10 minutes. Take off the heat and add the cheese beaten with the eggs. Season and turn into the pastry case.
3 Bake at 200°C/400°F (Gas Mark 6) on the second shelf from the top for 15–20 minutes or until the filling is golden. Serve with baked potatoes and salad.

Approximate cost of ingredients: £1.35

● To bake blind means to bake a pastry case without a filling. To prevent shrinkage stab with a fork, or put a piece of greaseproof paper (greased side down) on the bottom and fill with beans or dried peas.

Vegetable Curry

Ingredients	*Approximately*
2 carrots, grated	8p
1 stick celery, chopped	5p
1 green pepper, sliced	25p
Crushed garlic, to taste	10p
4 small onions, sliced	20p
30–45ml/2–3 tablespoons vegetable oil	
55g/2 oz mushrooms, sliced	15p
3 cooked potatoes	10p
15ml/1 tablespoon raisins	
395g/14 oz tin tomatoes	20p
25ml/5 teaspoons curry powder	5p
Salt	
30ml/2 tablespoons soya sauce	
15ml/1 tablespoon tomato purée	

Method

1 Sauté the vegetables in the oil beginning with the carrots, celery, pepper, garlic and onions, for 10 minutes.
2 Add the mushrooms, stir and add the potatoes and raisins. Add the tomatoes and stir in the curry powder, salt to taste and soya sauce.
3 Leave the mixture to simmer for 10 minutes then add the tomato purée, stir and simmer for a further 10 minutes. Serve hot with brown rice and salad.

Approximate cost of ingredients: £1.18

- A salad garnish, e.g., watercress or plain cucumber slices can suffice with a meal already containing plenty of vegetables.

● Stale bread can be freshened if brushed entirely in milk and baked moderately for 15 minutes. The crust will be crispened and the inside nicer than otherwise.

Bread and Cheese Pudding

Ingredients   *Approximately*
12 slices wholemeal bread, spread with margarine   25p
225g/½ lb grated cheese   70p
3 eggs   25p
425ml/¾ pint milk   20p
5ml/1 teaspoon mustard
Salt and freshly ground black pepper
7.5ml/½ tablespoon margarine or butter

Method
1   Make alternate layers of bread and cheese, starting with bread and ending with cheese, in a shallow ovenproof dish. Beat the eggs, milk, mustard and seasoning together and pour over the bread and cheese. Dot the top with flecks of margarine or butter and bake at 180°C/350°F (Gas Mark 4) for 20 minutes. Serve with salad.

Approximate cost of ingredients: £1.40

Spaghetti Neapolitan

Ingredients	*Approximately*
285g/10 oz wholewheat spaghetti	26p
4 small onions, sliced	20p
3 carrots, grated	15p
1 green pepper, chopped	25p
55g/2 oz mushrooms	15p
Crushed garlic, to taste	10p
15–30ml/1–2 tablespoons vegetable oil	
395g/14 oz tin tomatoes	20p
15ml/1 tablespoon tomato concentrate	
5ml/1 teaspoon mixed dried herbs	
15ml/1 tablespoon soya sauce	
Salt and freshly ground black pepper	

Method

1 Lower the spaghetti into 1.75 litres/3 pints of boiling salted water and cook until soft but not mushy (approximately 12 minutes) then drain.
2 Sauté the vegetables in oil until just tender. Add the tinned tomatoes, tomato concentrate, herbs, soya sauce and seasoning.
3 Cover and cook gently for 30 minutes adding a little more water if the sauce becomes too thick. Serve hot with spaghetti and salad.

Approximate cost of ingredients: £1.31

• Finish off old supplies of food before starting new ones.

Vegetable Pie

Ingredients	*Approximately*
340g/12 oz wholemeal self-raising flour	12p
170g/6 oz margarine	20p

Filling:

570ml/1 pint milk	26p
55g/2 oz flour	
2 carrots, sliced	10p
115g/4 oz frozen peas	9p
225g/½ lb boiled potatoes, cubed	10p
30–45ml/2–3 tablespoons vegetable oil	
Salt and freshly ground black pepper	
Milk, for glazing	

Method

1 Use the flour and margarine to make shortcrust pastry (see page 34). Use three-quarters of the pastry to line a pie dish or tin and keep the rest to make the lid.
2 Stir the milk gradually into the flour, bring to the boil stirring continually until the mixture has thickened to make a white sauce. Set aside.
3 Sauté the vegetables in oil starting with the carrots for 10 minutes. Add the peas and well drained potatoes and cook for a minute.
4 Stir in the sauce and seasoning and use to fill the pie case.
5 Roll out the rest of the pastry to make a lid. Lift on top of the pie, seal the edges and make a small incision in the lid (or prick a few holes with a fork).
6 Brush the top with milk and bake at 170°C/325°F (Gas Mark 3) for 20–25 minutes or until the pastry is cooked. Serve with baked potatoes and salad.

Approximate cost: 87p

Cheese and Vegetable Pie

Ingredients	*Approximately*
4 small onions, sliced	20p
15–30ml/1–2 tablespoons vegetable oil	
170g/6 oz spinach, rinsed and chopped	20p
455g/1 lb cooked potatoes, sliced or cubed	20p
Kernels from 1 corn on the cob, cooked	25p
115g/4 oz grated Cheddar	35p
570ml/1 pint Medium White Sauce (see page 37)	28p
Salt and freshly ground black pepper	

Pastry:

340g/¾ lb self-raising wholemeal flour	12p
170g/6 oz margarine	20p
A little milk	

Method

1   Sauté the onions in the oil until golden — about 5 minutes. Stir in the spinach and sauté a further 5 minutes.
2   Add the cooked potatoes and corn kernels. Add the cheese to the sauce and pour this over the vegetables. Stir well and season.
3   Make up the pastry using the flour and margarine and a little milk or water and use half to line a flan case or pie dish. Bake at 170°C/325°F (Gas Mark 3) for 10 minutes.
4   Spoon the vegetables into the case and top with a lid made from the remaining pastry.
5   Brush with milk and bake at 180°C/350°F (Gas Mark 4) on the third rung from the top for 20 minutes until the pastry is golden brown. Serve with baked potatoes and salad.

Approximate cost of ingredients: £1.80

Potato Pie

Ingredients	*Approximately*
115g/4 oz streaky bacon	25p
15ml/1 tablespoon vegetable oil	
4 small onions or 1 large onion, sliced	20p
30ml/2 tablespoons flour	
570ml/1 pint milk	26p
Salt and freshly grated black pepper	
Freshly grated nutmeg	
680g/1½ lb cooked potatoes, thickly sliced	15p

Pastry:

340g/¾ lb self-raising wholemeal flour	12p
170g/6 oz margarine	20p
A little milk	

Method

1 Chop the bacon and fry in the oil. Add the onion and cook until lightly golden.
2 Add the flour, stir well and slowly add the milk. Bring to the boil stirring continually to make a smooth sauce. Season with salt, pepper and nutmeg.
3 Add the cooked potatoes, take off the heat and set aside.
4 Make the pastry using the flour, margarine and a little water to bind the dough. Use half to line a pie dish and bake at 170°C/325°F (Gas Mark 3) for 10 minutes.
5 Spoon in the potato mixture. Cover with a thin lid made from the rest of the pastry. Brush with milk and bake at 180°C/350°F (Gas Mark 4) for 20 minutes until the pastry is golden brown. Serve with Brussels sprouts and salad.

Approximate cost of ingredients: £1.18

● Make a note when supplies of anything are running low. This should help reduce the number of your shopping trips.

Popeye Pasties

Ingredients	*Approximately*
285g/10 oz wholemeal self-raising flour	10p
140g/5 oz margarine	15p
A little water	
3 potatoes, cooked and mashed	15p
285g/10 oz cream cheese	£1.00
170g/6 oz cooked spinach, chopped	20p
15ml/1 tablespoon chopped chives	
45ml/3 tablespoons milk	
Salt and freshly ground black pepper	
1 small onion, chopped	8p

Method
1 Make pastry from the flour and margarine and a little water (see page 34). With floured hands, shape the pastry into a large roll about 4cm/1½ inches thick. Cut the roll into 2–3cm/1- inch pieces and roll each one out to a circle. Sprinkle them with flour and leave ready to fill.
2 Combine the potatoes, cream cheese, spinach, chopped chives and milk. Season and add the onion.
3 Put a spoonful of the mixture into the centre of each circle of pastry. Dampen the edges with a little milk, fold the pastries over and press them together so that the filling cannot escape.
4 Brush with milk and bake at 170°C/325°F (Gas Mark 3) for 20 minutes until golden brown. Serve with sour cream or yogurt if liked, baked potatoes and salad.

Approximate cost of ingredients: £1.68

• Food not consumed should be stored in the fridge (it will keep for 2–3 days) and used as soon as possible e.g., quiche will serve re-heated as lunch the following day (waste not want not).

Lentil Flan

(Serves 5)

Ingredients	*Approximately*
Pastry:	
225g/$\frac{1}{2}$ lb wholemeal flour	8p
115g/4 oz margarine	12p
A little cold water or milk	
Filling:	
250g/9 oz red split lentils	30p
850ml/1$\frac{1}{2}$ pints water	
4 small onions, sliced	20p
3–4 carrots, grated	15p
Crushed garlic, to taste	10p
15–30ml/1–2 tablespoons vegetable oil	
Juice of $\frac{1}{2}$–1 lemon	10p
30ml/2 tablespoons tomato concentrate	
Salt and freshly ground black pepper	
115g/4 oz grated cheese	35p

Method

1 Make up the pastry by rubbing the fat into the flour and bringing to a dough with a little water. Use to line a flan tin or pie dish and bake at 170°C/325°F (Gas Mark 3) for 10 minutes.

2 Bring the lentils to the boil in the water and simmer, stirring occasionally over a low heat without a lid, for about 15 minutes until soft but not runny (if runny, simmer for a further 10 minutes, stirring continually).

3 Meanwhile, sauté the onion, carrots and garlic in the oil in a covered pan over a low heat for 10–15 minutes.

4 Add the cooked lentils, lemon juice, tomato concentrate and seasoning. Stir well and spoon into the pre-baked pastry case.

5 Bake at 200°C/400°F (Gas Mark 6) for 15 minutes then sprinkle with the grated cheese and continue to bake at 170°C/325°F (Gas Mark 3) until the cheese has melted. Serve with baked potatoes and salad.

Approximate cost of ingredients: £1.40

Cowboy Beans

Ingredients	Approximately
300g/11 oz red kidney beans	45p
1.4 litres/2½ pints water	
4 onions, sliced	20p
1 green pepper, sliced	25p
Crushed garlic, to taste	10p
15ml/1 tablespoon vegetable oil	
55g/2 oz mushrooms, sliced	15p
395g/14 oz tin tomatoes	20p
10ml/2 teaspoons yeast extract or 30ml/2 tablespoons soya sauce	
2.5ml–5ml/½–1 teaspoon cayenne pepper	
15ml/1 tablespoon tomato purée	
Salt	

Method

1 Soak the beans overnight and simmer in the water in a pan with a tight fitting lid for 90 minutes, or pressure cook at 15 lb pressure for 15 minutes. Or, bring the unsoaked beans to the boil and simmer for 2½ hours in a saucepan with a tight fitting lid. Do not add salt until the beans are cooked and use only soft cooked beans — see note page 30.
2 Sauté the onions, pepper and garlic in the oil for 10 minutes over a low heat in a lidded frying pan. Add the mushrooms, stir then add the cooked beans and tinned tomatoes.
3 Flavour with yeast extract or soya sauce, cayenne pepper, tomato purée and salt. Stir then sauté for a further 15 minutes. Serve with baked potatoes or rice and salad.

Approximate cost of ingredients: £1.35

Variation:

Mexican Beans

Brown 225–455g/½–1 lb mince, add the above vegetables and sauté as before etc., using the above method.

Approximate cost of ingredients: £1.95–£2.29

Lentil Loaf

Ingredients	*Approximately*
285g/10 oz red split lentils	40p
1.1 litres/2 pints water	
4 small onions, sliced	20p
3–4 carrots, grated	15p
15–30ml/1–2 tablespoons vegetable oil	
115g/4 oz sage and onion stuffing (dry)	30p
7.5ml/$\frac{1}{2}$ tablespoon tomato purée	
Salt and freshly ground black pepper	

Method

1 Bring the lentils to the boil in the water, lower the heat and simmer without a lid for 15 minutes.
2 Simmer the onions and carrots in the oil over a low heat in a covered saucepan — about 10–15 minutes.
3 Add the cooked lentils which should be soft but not runny. (If runny, simmer them for a further 10 minutes, stirring continually.)
4 Add the sage and onion stuffing and if the mixture seems too dry add 140–285ml/$\frac{1}{4}$–$\frac{1}{2}$ pint of hot water. (The mixture should cling onto a wooden spoon when it is shaken.)
5 Add the tomato purée and seasoning and turn into a greased oven-proof dish. Bake at 190°C/375°F (Gas Mark 5) for about 20 minutes until crisp on top. Serve with baked potatoes and salad.

Approximate cost of ingredients: £1.05

● Fruit and vegetables are at their best and cheapest when they are in season.

Vegetable Risotto

Ingredients	Approximately
285g/10 oz brown rice	40p
1.1 litres/2 pints salted water	
3 carrots, grated	15p
3 onions, sliced	16p
2 sticks celery, chopped	10p
Crushed garlic, to taste	10p
15–30ml/1–2 tablespoons vegetable oil	
115g/4 oz frozen peas	8p
395g/14 oz tin tomatoes	20p
15–30ml/1–2 tablespoons soya sauce	
7.5ml/$\frac{1}{2}$ tablespoon tomato purée	
Salt and freshly ground black pepper	

Method

1 Cook the rice in salted water following the recipe on page 30.
2 Whilst the rice is cooking, sauté the carrots, onions, celery and garlic in the oil for 10–15 minutes. Add the peas, tomatoes, stir in the soya sauce and tomato purée.
3 Add the cooked rice and simmer gently for 10 minutes, stirring occasionally. Season to taste. Serve with salad.

Approximate cost of ingredients: £1.19

Rice 'n' Peas

Ingredients	Approximately
170g/6 oz red kidney beans	23p
1.7 litres/3 pints water	
300g/11 oz brown rice	40p
3 carrots, grated	15p
3 onions, sliced	20p
Garlic, to taste, crushed	10p
1 green pepper, sliced	25p
30–40ml/2–3 tablespoons vegetable oil	
395g/14 oz tin tomatoes	20p
10ml/2 teaspoons yeast extract	6p
Salt	
Cayenne pepper	

Method

1 Bring the beans to the boil in the water and boil vigorously for 10 minutes then cover and simmer gently for 2 hours.
2 Add the rice, stir and cover and cook for 20 minutes until tender.
3 Sauté the vegetables in the oil for about 15 minutes starting with the carrot, onion and garlic then adding the pepper.
4 Add the tinned tomatoes and yeast extract with salt and cayenne pepper.
5 Add the cooked beans and rice, stir, cover and cook gently for 10–15 minutes. Serve with salad.

Approximate cost of ingredients: £1.59

Note: The peas referred to in the recipe title are in fact beans.

Sautéed (Stir-Fried) Vegetables

Basically any combination of vegetables can be sautéed but lighter vegetables like mushrooms, sweetcorn, peas and peppers are favoured.

Ingredients	*Approximately*
2–3 tablespoons vegetable oil	
3 carrots, chopped and sliced lengthways	15p
225g/8 oz courgettes, sliced lengthways	30p
225g/8 oz beansprouts	20p
3 tablespoons soya sauce plus ½ pint water *or*	
1 tablespoon yeast extract plus ½ pint water	5p
Salt and freshly ground black pepper	

Method
1 Start by heating the oil in the pan then add the carrots. Stir, cover and sauté gently for 10 minutes.
2 Add the courgettes, stir and cover, and shortly afterwards add the beansprouts.
3 Stir well, cover and sauté for around 5 minutes before adding the stock. Season to taste, cover and cook for a further 5–10 minutes. Serve with hot rice, etc.

Approximate cost of ingredients: 70p

Fish Pie I

Ingredients	*Approximately*
680g/1½ lb filleted fish	£1.50
10ml/2 teaspoons chopped parsley	
1 onion, grated or finely chopped	8p
2 eggs	16p
570ml/1 pint milk	26p

Salt and freshly ground black pepper
30ml/2 tablespoons breadcrumbs
55g/2 oz margarine or butter   6p
55g/2 oz grated cheese   20p

Method
1 Poach or sauté the fish, cool, flake and layer into a greased pie dish with the parsley and onion, starting with fish.
2 Beat the eggs, milk and seasoning and pour over the fish.
3 Bake at 180°C/350°F (Gas Mark 4) until the top feels firm. Cover with a mixture of breadcrumbs, margarine and cheese. Grill for 3–4 minutes until the cheese is golden brown.
4 Serve with baked potatoes and salad.

Approximate cost of ingredients: £2.26

Fish Pie II

Ingredients   *Approximately*
1 corn on the cob   25p
455g/1 lb cooked fish   £1.00
285ml/½ pint medium white sauce   14p
900g/2 lb potato, mashed with a little margarine   20p
Salt and freshly ground black pepper

Method
1 Strip the kernels from the corn and boil in unsalted water for 10 minutes. Drain well.
2 Flake the fish into a pie dish. Add the corn. Pour over the white sauce.
3 Season the mashed potato and use to cover the pie. Bake at 180°C/350°F (Gas Mark 4) for 15 minutes or until piping hot.

Approximate cost of ingredients: £1.59

Note:
Use mushrooms or other vegetables when corn is not available.
Serve with lightly-boiled vegetables and salad.

Baked Mackerel

Ingredients   *Approximately*
2 large mackerel   £2.00
30ml/2 tablespoons vegetable oil

Method
1   Brush the cleaned mackerel with oil and place them side by
    side in an oven-proof dish. Bake on the third rung at
    180°C/350°F (Gas Mark 4) for approximately 35 minutes.
    Alternatively, surround the fish with sliced onion and bake, or
    stuff cleaned, but unsplit, mackerel with 115g/4 oz of sautéed
    mushrooms bound with a little flour and seasoned with salt
    and pepper.
2   Serve with baked potatoes and salad.

Approximate cost of ingredients:£2.00

Spicy Mackerel

Ingredients   *Approximately*
1.1 litres/2 pints water
1 sprig parsley
15ml/1 tablespoon lemon juice   5p
1 carrot, sliced   5p
1 onion, sliced   8p
Salt and freshly ground black pepper
2 mackerels, filleted   £1.50
30g/1 oz margarine or butter   3p
30g/1 oz flour
5ml/1 teaspoon curry powder

Method
1   Bring the water, parsley, lemon juice, carrot, onion and
    seasoning slowly to the boil and simmer for 5 minutes.
2   Add the fish and cook gently until tender. Remove the fish and
    keep warm.

3 Make a sauce by melting the margarine or butter, stirring in the flour and cooking for 1 minute. Slowly add the strained stock and curry powder and stir until smooth and creamy.
4 Return the cooked fish and serve hot with brown rice and salad.

Approximate cost of ingredients: £1.71

Fish Curry

Ingredients	Approximately
455g/1 lb filleted fish (mackerel)	80p
15ml/1 tablespoon vegetable oil	
55g/2 oz margarine or butter	6p
2 onions, chopped	16p
1 eating apple, peeled and chopped	10p
30ml/2 tablespoons flour	
285ml/$\frac{1}{2}$ pint stock or 5ml/1 teaspoon yeast extract with water	5p
22.5ml/1$\frac{1}{2}$ tablespoons curry powder	
140ml/$\frac{1}{4}$ pint top of the milk	7p
15ml/1 tablespoon lemon juice	
30g/1 oz desiccated coconut	7p
Salt	

Method
1 Cut the fish into 2cm/1-inch pieces and fry them for a few minutes in the oil. Remove them from the pan, add the margarine or butter and fry the onions and apple for a few minutes.
2 Stir in the flour and stock. Stir and add the curry powder and cook for 10 minutes.
3 Pour in the milk, lemon juice, coconut and salt and cook for 2–3 minutes before adding the fish.
4 Simmer gently for 30 minutes or more and serve with brown rice and salad.

Approximate cost of ingredients: £1.31

Fish Cakes

Ingredients	*Approximately*
455g/1 lb cooked filleted fish	£1.00
30–45ml/2–3 tablespoons vegetable oil	
900g/2 lb potatoes, cooked	20p
30g/1 oz margarine	3p
5ml/1 teaspoon tomato concentrate	
5ml/1 teaspoon yeast extract	5p
2 slices wholemeal bread	4p
1 egg	8p
Salt and freshly ground black pepper	
Flour, for shaping	

Method

1 Sauté the fish in a little of the oil until flaky.
2 Mash the potatoes and mix with the fish, margarine, tomato concentrate and yeast extract.
3 Grate or blend the bread to make crumbs and add to the mixture with the egg and seasoning.
4 Form into small cakes and roll them in a little flour. Fry the fish cakes on both sides in the remaining oil or bake in a little oil at 200°C/400°F (Gas Mark 6) until crisp and brown.
5 Serve with cauliflower or a suitable vegetable and salad.

Approximate cost of ingredients: £1.40

Macaroni Chicken

Ingredients	*Approximately*
225g/½ lb macaroni	25p
1 chicken piece, cooked	£1.15
2 carrots, grated	10p
2 onions, sliced	16p
Crushed garlic, to taste	10p
115g/4 oz frozen peas	8p
30–45ml/2–3 tablespoons vegetable oil	
15ml/1 tablespoon soya sauce	
395g/14 oz tin tomatoes	20p
2.5ml/½ teaspoon cayenne pepper	
Salt	
15ml/1 tablespoon tomato purée	

Method

1 Bring 1.75 litres/3 pints of water with 5ml/1 teaspoon salt to the boil and add the macaroni. Stir, cover and cook until soft but not mushy — about 12 minutes. Drain.
2 Cut the flesh from the cooked chicken into bite-sized pieces. Sauté the vegetables in the oil for about 10 minutes then add the soya sauce, the chicken and the tomatoes. Season with cayenne pepper and salt and stir in the tomato purée.
3 Cook over a low heat for 1–2 minutes. Add the macaroni and cook for a further 5–10 minutes. Serve hot with a simple salad.

Approximate cost of ingredients: £2.04

Chicken Casserole

Ingredients	Approximately
1 chicken piece	£1.15
Seasoned flour	
30ml/2 tablespoons vegetable oil	
455g/1 lb potatoes, chopped	10p
2 carrots, sliced	10p
2 onions, sliced	16p
Crushed garlic, to taste	10p
570ml/1 pint stock or 10ml/2 teaspoons yeast extract and water	10p
30ml/2 tablespoons fruit juice	
7.5ml/$\frac{1}{2}$ tablespoon tomato purée	
115g/4 oz frozen peas	8p

Method

1 Coat the chicken with seasoned flour and brown in the vegetable oil. Put it into an oven-proof casserole with all the vegetables except the peas.
2 Mix the stock and fruit juice with the tomato purée and pour over the vegetables. Bake at 220°C/425°F (Gas Mark 7) for 30 minutes.
3 Lift out the chicken, remove the flesh and cut it into bite-sized pieces. Return these to the vegetables.
4 Add the peas and cook for a further 30 minutes. Serve with dumplings.

Approximate cost of ingredients: £1.79

Chicken Curry with Vegetables

Ingredients	*Approximately*
1 chicken quarter	£1.00
1 stick celery, chopped	5p
4 small onions, sliced	20p
Crushed garlic, to taste	10p
1 green pepper, sliced	25p
55g/2 oz mushrooms, sliced	15p
30–45ml/2–3 tablespoons vegetable oil	
25ml/5 teaspoons curry powder	5p
395g/14 oz tin tomatoes	20p
30ml/2 tablespoons soya sauce	
Salt	
15ml/1 tablespoon tomato purée	

Method

1 Sauté the chicken until cooked – about 25 minutes. Cool and remove the flesh and cut it into bite-sized pieces.
2 Sauté the vegetables in oil for about 10 minutes. Stir in the curry powder, tinned tomatoes and chicken.
3 Add the soya sauce and salt to taste then simmer for 15 minutes, stirring occasionally.
4 Add the tomato purée and cook for a further 10 minutes. Serve with brown rice and salad.

Approximate cost of ingredients: £2.00

Chicken and Vegetable Pie

Ingredients	*Approximately*
1 chicken quarter	£1.00
4 small onions, sliced	20p
15ml/1 tablespoon vegetable oil	
1 corn on the cob (substitute carrots when corn is not available)	25p
170g/6 oz spinach, rinsed and chopped	20p
570ml/1 pint medium white sauce	28p
Salt and freshly ground black pepper	

Pastry:

340g/$\frac{3}{4}$ lb wholemeal self-raising flour	12p
170g/6 oz margarine	20p
A little milk	

Method

1 Fry the chicken until cooked, about 30 minutes. Cook, remove the flesh and cut into bite-sized pieces.
2 Sauté the onions in the vegetable oil for about 5 minutes. Cut the corn kernels from the cob and add them to the onion. Stir well and add the spinach.
3 Stir fry for a further 5 minutes then add to the chicken and white sauce. Stir well and season to taste.
4 Make up the pastry from the flour and margarine bound with a little water and use half to line a flan case or pie plate. Bake at 170°C/325°F (Gas Mark 3) for 10 minutes.
5 Fill with the chicken mixture and cover with a lid made from the remaining pastry. Make a small slit in the centre of the lid, brush all over with milk and continue to bake at 180°C/350°F (Gas Mark 4) for 20 minutes until the pastry is golden brown. Serve with baked potatoes and salad.

Approximate cost of ingredients: £2.25

Spicy Spare Rib Chops

Ingredients   **Approximately**
Sauce:
10ml/2 teaspoons salt
30ml/2 tablespoons sugar
15ml/1 tablespoon vinegar
30ml/2 tablespoons soya sauce
150ml/5 fl oz apple juice   5p
2.5ml/½ teaspoon cayenne pepper
565–680g/1¼–1½ lb spare rib chops   £1.80
15ml/1 tablespoon wholemeal flour

Method
1 Mix the sauce ingredients together in a heavy-based saucepan
   or casserole. Add 285ml/½ pint water, stir.
2 Cut the chops into large pieces and add to the sauce. Bring to
   the boil, cover and simmer gently for about 45 minutes turning
   the pieces occasionally.
3 When the meat is tender, sprinkle the flour into the sauce,
   stirring continually until the sauce thickens. Serve with rice
   or spaghetti.

Approximate cost of ingredients: £1.85

● To remove grease from soup or gravy dip in small
  pieces of clean tissue to absorb the fat.

Pork and Beans

Ingredients	Approximately
250g/9 oz blackeye beans	35p
850ml/1½ pints water	
225g/½ lb spare rib pork chops	60p
1 large onion, sliced	8p
Crushed garlic, to taste	10p
15ml/1 tablespoon vegetable oil	
30ml/2 tablespoons soya sauce	
Freshly ground black pepper	
5ml/1 teaspoon brown sugar	
5ml/1 teaspoon vinegar	
395g/14 oz tin tomatoes	20p

Method

1 Boil the beans in the water until cooked — about 25–30 minutes.
2 Fry the chops lightly on both sides.
3 Add the onion and garlic with the oil if needed and fry until the onions are golden.
4 Add the soya sauce, pepper, brown sugar and vinegar. Cook for a further 5 minutes then turn the mixture into a deep oven-proof casserole.
5 Add the tomatoes. Cover and bake at 180°C/350°F (Gas Mark 4) for about 15 minutes. Serve with potatoes or rice and salad.

Approximate cost of ingredients: £1.33

Sweet and Sour Pork

Ingredients	Approximately
455g/1 lb belly pork, skinned and cubed	90p
30ml/2 tablespoons vegetable oil	
140ml/¼ pint water	
22.5ml/1½ tablespoons brown sugar	

15ml/1 tablespoon soya sauce
10ml/2 teaspoons vinegar
Cornflour, to thicken

Method
1 Fry the pork cubes in oil. Drain and set aside.
2 Put the water, sugar, soya sauce and vinegar into a saucepan
   and bring to the boil. Thicken lightly with a little cornflour
   mixed with water.
3 Add the pork and simmer for 10 minutes. Serve with brown rice
   and stir-fried vegetables.

Approximate cost of ingredients: £1.00

Kidney and Bacon Pilaff

Ingredients	Approximately
285g/10 oz brown rice	40p
1.1 litres/2 pints salted water	
340g/ $\frac{3}{4}$ lb kidney	75p
115g/4 oz streaky bacon	25p
1 large onion, sliced	8p
115g/4 oz mushrooms, sliced	30p
285ml/$\frac{1}{2}$ pint stock or water with 5ml/1 teaspoon yeast	
extract 15ml/1 tablespoon wholemeal flour	

Method
1 Cook the rice in salted water following the recipe on page 30.
2 Whilst the rice is cooking, halve and remove the kidney cores
   and cut the kidney and bacon into small pieces. Fry them,
   together with the onion until the onion is soft, adding a little
   vegetable oil if necessary.
3 Add the mushrooms and sauté for 1 minute. Stir in the stock
   and simmer until the ingredients are tender.
4 Sprinkle on the flour and stir into the pilaff continually until
   the sauce thickens. Serve with a border of rice and a salad.

Approximate cost of ingredients: £1.78

Meat Loaf

Ingredients	*Approximately*
455g/1 lb minced beef	94p
15ml/1 tablespoon vegetable oil	
3 carrots, grated	15p
2 small onions, sliced	16p
4 cloves garlic, crushed	10p
2 large slices wholemeal bread	10p
115g/4 oz sage and onion stuffing	30p
7.5ml/$\frac{1}{2}$ tablespoon tomato purée	
5ml/1 teaspoon yeast extract	5p
Salt and freshly ground black pepper	

Method

1 Brown the mince in vegetable oil. Add the carrots and onions, cover and continue to simmer over a low heat for 10–15 minutes. Add the crushed garlic.

2 Meanwhile, grind the bread into crumbs and add to the mince with the sage and onion stuffing. Stir well and if the mixture seems too dry add 140–285ml ($\frac{1}{4}$–$\frac{1}{2}$ pint) hot water.

3 Add the tomato purée, yeast extract and seasoning.

4 Turn the mixture into a greased oven-proof dish, brush the top with oil and bake at 190°C/375°F (Gas Mark 5) for 20 minutes until crisp on top. Serve with baked potatoes and salad.

Approximate cost of ingredients: £1.80

● Make a mock beef stock out of a little onion, carrot, celery, grated ginger, crushed garlic and soya sauce. Simply simmer for 10 minutes.

Rice with Mince

Ingredients	*Approximately*
285g/10 oz brown rice	40p
1.1litres/2 pints salted water	
225g/8 oz minced beef	70p
15–30ml/1–2 tablespoons vegetable oil	
3 onions, sliced	15p
Crushed garlic, to taste	10p
Finely chopped parsley	5p
Salt and freshly ground black pepper	

Method
1 Cook the rice in the salted water following the recipe on page 30.
2 Brown the mince in hot oil. Add the onion and garlic and sauté for 5 minutes.
3 Add the parsley and sauté for a further 5–10 minutes. Add the cooked rice, stir and season. Serve with tomato sauce and salad.

Approximate cost of ingredients: £1.40

Liver and Mushrooms I

Ingredients	*Approximately*
1 large onion, sliced	8p
30ml/2 tablespoons vegetable oil	
115g/4 oz mushrooms, sliced	30p
455g/1 lb liver of choice, chopped small and rolled in flour	88p
2.5ml/½ teaspoon marjoram	
Salt and freshly ground black pepper	
285ml/½ pint stock or water mixed with 5ml/1 teaspoon yeast extract	

Method

1 Fry the onion in the oil until golden. Add the mushrooms and liver and fry slowly for 5 minutes.
2 Sprinkle with majoram and season to taste. Pour on the stock and cook over a low heat until the liver is tender. Serve with wholewheat macaroni or noodles.

Approximate cost of ingredients: £1.26

Liver and Mushrooms II

Ingredients	*Approximately*
Crushed garlic, to taste	10p
15–30ml/1–2 tablespoons vegetable oil	
455g/1 lb lamb's liver of choice, thinly sliced	£1.05
Freshly ground black pepper	
115g/4 oz mushrooms, sliced	30p

Method

1 Sauté the garlic in oil for 5 minutes. Add the liver and sprinkle liberally with black pepper.
2 Prick the liver with a fork and fry gently on both sides for about 10 minutes.

3   Add the mushrooms, stir and cover. Continue to cook gently
    for a further 5 minutes. Serve with potatoes or rice and salad.

Approximate cost of ingredients: £1.45

Baked Liver and Bacon

Ingredients	*Approximately*
15–30ml/1–2 tablespoons vegetable oil	
455g/1 lb thinly sliced liver of choice	88p
8 rashers streaky bacon	50p

Method
1   Grease a shallow baking dish with the oil and coat liver on both
    sides with the oil. Arrange liver in dish and place the bacon on
    top.
2   Bake in a moderate oven 180°C/350°F (Gas Mark 4) until
    bacon is crisp, approximately 15–20 minutes. Serve with
    baked potatoes and salad.

Approximate cost of ingredients: £1.38

Toad in the Hole

Ingredients	*Approximately*
Batter:	
140g/5 oz plain flour	5p
Pinch salt	
1–2 eggs	16p
425ml/¾ pint milk	20p
455g/1 lb low-fat sausages	£1.05

Method

1 To make the batter, sift the flour and salt into a basin, break in the egg(s) and stir them into the flour gradually adding the milk until the batter is like thick cream. Beat for 10 minutes. Alternatively, mix the batter in a blender. If possible, leave the batter to stand for 1 hour.

2 Prick the sausages and heat in a baking tin in a 220°C/425°F (Gas Mark 7) oven until the fat runs. Pour over the batter and continue to bake for about 30 minutes until the batter is well risen and a rich golden brown.

3 Serve at once with baked potatoes and salad.

Approximate cost of ingredients: £1.46

Spaghetti Bolognaise

Ingredients	Approximately
225g/½ lb minced beef	65p
15ml/1 tablespoon vegetable oil	
1 green pepper, sliced	25p
4 onions, sliced	16p
Crushed garlic, to taste	10p
55g/2 oz mushrooms, sliced	15p
2.5ml/½ teaspoon mixed herbs	
395g/14 oz tinned tomatoes	20p
Salt and freshly ground black pepper	
15ml/1 tablespoon soya sauce	
7.5ml/½ tablespoon tomato purée	
15ml/1 tablespoon wholemeal flour	
285g/10 oz wholewheat spaghetti	26p
10ml/2 teaspoons salt	

Method

1 Fry the beef in the oil over a high heat until brown. Add the pepper, onion and garlic, cover with a lid and simmer for 10 minutes.
2 Add the sliced mushrooms and herbs and sauté for 5 minutes. Add the tomatoes, seasoning, soya sauce and tomato purée.
3 Stir well then sprinkle with the flour and stir again.
4 Leave over a low heat and bring 1.75 litres/3 pints of water to the boil with the 10ml/2 teaspoons salt. When the water boils, add the spaghetti and cook until soft but not mushy — about 12 minutes.
5 Drain the spaghetti and serve with the hot sauce and a simple salad.

Approximate cost of ingredients: £1.87

Roast Chicken

Ingredients	*Approximately*
1 roasting chicken without giblets	£2.50
115g/4 oz sage and onion stuffing (made up)	30p

Baste:
1 teaspoon salt
2 teaspoons soya sauce
½ teaspoon sugar
1 teaspoon vinegar
2 teaspoons vegetable oil

Method

1   Place the chicken in a roasting tin. Remove any surplus fat from leg cavity and fill with the sage and onion stuffing.
2   Mix the baste ingredients, adding the oil last, and brush the chicken all over with it. Bake at 200°C/400°F (Gas Mark 6) on the third rung from the top for approximately 1 hour 15 minutes, till the juices burst and the fat runs and the skin is browned and crispy.

Approximate cost of ingredients: £2.80

Note:
To avoid the spread of food poisoning care must be taken to make sure that uncooked chicken is well wrapped when stored in the refrigerator and not directly in contact with other food. Also, any worktops used for preparing chicken must be washed down thoroughly.

● The bones left over from a chicken or Christmas turkey make excellent stock. Simply boil with any left-over bits of vegetables i.e., carrots, onions, celery etc., for about 25 minutes.

5
Salads

Green Salad

Ingredients	Approximately
½ lettuce	15p
½ bunch watercress	15p
Cucumber, sliced	10p
½ green pepper, sliced	15p
Small spring onion, finely chopped	8p
A few green olives	10p

Method
1. Rinse and drain the lettuce and watercress. Chop the lettuce and add other ingredients.
2. Top with a simple dressing of 5ml/1 teaspoon salt, vinegar and oil mixed in an egg cup and with a liberal sprinkling of freshly ground pepper.

Approximate cost: 73p

- Sad and limp watercress can be revived by standing upright in cold water.

Orange and Onion Salad

Ingredients	*Approximately*
3 oranges	36p
3 onions, chopped	24p

Dressing:
15ml/1 tablespoon vegetable oil
10ml/2 teaspoons vinegar
5ml/1 teaspoon lemon juice
2.5ml/½ teaspoon chopped tarragon
2.5ml/½ teaspoon sugar

Method
1 Peel the oranges removing white pith. Slice into rounds, removing the seeds.
2 Combine with the onions and add the salad dressing.

Approximate cost: 60p

Rice Salad

Ingredients	*Approximately*
300g/11 oz brown rice	40p
2 carrots, grated	10p
115g/4 oz white cabbage, shredded	8p
1 small onion, minced	5p
115g/4 oz cooked green peas	8p
15ml/1 tablespoon raisins	

Dressing:
5ml/1 teaspoon salt
15ml/1 tablespoon soya sauce
15ml/1 tablespoon vinegar
2.5ml/½ teaspoon mustard powder
15ml/1 tablespoon vegetable oil

Method
1 Boil the rice until tender but not mushy (see page 30).
2 Add the other ingredients to hot rice and season with the
   mixed dressing. Serve hot or cold.

Approximate cost: 71p

Potato Salad

Ingredients	*Approximately*
900g/2 lb potatoes, cooked and cubed	20p
1 onion, chopped	8p
2 stalks celery, chopped	10p
2 hard boiled eggs, sliced	16p
Finely chopped parsley	5p

Dressing:

115g/4 oz cream cheese	37p
15ml/1 tablespoon vegetable oil	
15ml/1 tablespoon vinegar	
Salt and freshly ground black pepper	

Method
1 Cook the potatoes until just tender but not soft. Cube and
   combine with the remaining ingredients whilst hot, adding the
   salad dressing last.
2 Chill and serve.

Approximate cost: 96p

Redbean Salad

Ingredients	Approximately
300g/11 oz red kidney beans	45p
1 green pepper, chopped	25p
2 stalks celery, chopped	10p
1 onion, finely chopped	8p
Crushed garlic, to taste	10p

Dressing:
15ml/1 tablespoon lemon juice
15ml/1 tablespoon vegetable oil
Salt and freshly ground black pepper

Method
1 Cook the beans as outlined on page 30.
2 Mix all the ingredients together with the dressing ingredients, whilst the beans are still hot. Chill and serve.

Approximate cost: 98p

Curried Rice Salad

Ingredients	Approximately
300g/11 oz brown rice	40p
1 green pepper, chopped	25p
2 sticks celery	10p
2 carrots, grated	10p
1 small onion, chopped finely	8p
1 small apple, grated	10p

Dressing:
5ml/1 teaspoon salt,
15ml/1 tablespoon soya sauce
15ml/1 tablespoon vinegar
10–15ml/2–3 teaspoons curry powder
15ml/1 tablespoon vegetable oil

Method
1 Boil the rice until soft but not mushy.
2 Add ingredients to hot rice and season with the dressing.
   Serve hot or cold.

Approximate cost: £1.23

Macaroni Salad

Ingredients	*Approximately*
225g/½ lb macaroni	25p
115g/4 oz cooked peas or sweet corn	8p
55g/2 oz mushrooms, sliced	15p
2 stalks celery chopped	10p
Finely chopped parsley	5p

Dressing:

150g/5 oz carton natural yogurt	23p
15ml/1 tablespoon vegetable oil	
15ml/1 tablespoon orange juice	
Salt and freshly ground black pepper	

Method
1 Cook macaroni as outlined on page 95. Combine with the rest
   of the ingredients and the dressing whilst the macaroni is hot.
2 Chill and serve. Alternatively add tinned tuna (drained) to the
   ingredients when cold.

Approximate cost: 86p

Mackerel Salad

Ingredients	*Approximately*
1 medium mackerel	£1.00
½ round lettuce, rinsed	15p
½ bunch watercress, rinsed and chopped	15p
1 onion, finely chopped	8p
1 carrot, grated	5p
Piece cucumber, sliced	5p
A few olives	10p

Dressing:
15ml/1 tablespoon lemon juice
5ml/1 teaspoon mustard powder
15ml/1 tablespoon vegetable oil
Salt and freshly ground black pepper

Method
1 If not using filleted fish, bake in a moderate oven preheated to 180°C/350°F (Gas Mark 4) for about 20 minutes and remove bones. If filleted sauté till flaky.
2 Marinate for up to 1 hour in the dressing then add other ingredients and mix well.

Approximate cost: £1.58

Chicken Salad

Ingredients	*Approximately*
2 pieces chicken, cooked	£1.80
2 carrots, grated	10p
½ green pepper	15p
2 stalks celery, chopped	10p
Piece cucumber, sliced	5p
Few mushrooms, sliced	5p
A tomato, sliced	10p
A few raisins	

Dressing:

150g/5 oz carton natural yogurt	23p
60ml/4 tablespoons top of the milk	
5ml/1 teaspoon lemon juice	
15ml/1 tablespoon vegetable oil	
Salt and freshly ground black pepper	

Method

1 If not using cooked chicken, sauté chicken for about 30 minutes in a covered pan, turning occasionally.
2 Remove meat from the bone and marinate for up to 1 hour in a mixed dressing of 5ml/1 teaspoon salt, 2.5ml/½ teaspoon black pepper, 2.5ml/½ teaspoon mustard powder, 2.5ml/½ teaspoon sugar, 15ml/1 tablespoon lemon juice or vinegar and 10ml/2 teaspoons oil.
3 Drain if necessary and combine with other ingredients, plus the yogurt dressing.

Approximate cost: £2.58

- Do not buy more food than can be used while it is still in first class condition. Green vegetables and perishables should be bought fresh daily.

6

Desserts

Bread and Butter Pudding

Ingredients	Approximately
6 slices wholemeal bread, spread with margarine	13p
115g/4 oz sultanas	12p
2 eggs	17p
55g/2 oz brown sugar	5p
570ml/1 pint milk	23p

Method

1. Arrange layers of bread and sultanas, ending with a layer of bread, in a greased, oven-proof pie dish (bread should only half fill the dish).
2. Beat the eggs, sugar and milk and pour over the bread.
3. Bake at 180°C/350°F (Gas Mark 4) for 1 hour.

Approximate cost of ingredients: 70p

Humble Crumble

Ingredients	Approximately
455g/1 lb cooking apples, plums or rhubarb	42p
15ml/1 tablespoon demerara sugar	2p
150–300ml/5–10 fl oz water	
115g/4 oz margarine	12p
170g/6 oz wholemeal flour	6p
170g/6 oz porridge oats	12p
85g/3 oz demerara sugar	12p
15ml/1 tablespoon vegetable oil	

Method

1 Rinse, quarter and core the apples. Slice them into a shallow oven-proof dish, packing the slices in tightly.
2 Spinkle with 15ml/1 tablespoon sugar and add the water.
3 Make a crumble topping by rubbing the fat into the dry ingredients. Add a little oil if the mixture still feels dry after mixing. Spoon the crumble over the fruit and bake at 190°C/ 375°F (Gas Mark 5) for 25–30 minutes or until the fruit starts to bubble up and the crumble topping turns brown. Serve with custard, cream, ice cream, or yogurt.

Approximate cost of ingredients: 86p

Fruity Pie

Ingredients	*Approximately*
Pastry:	
340g/¾ lb self-raising wholemeal flour	12p
170g/6 oz margarine	20p
A little milk or water	
Filling:	
455g/1 lb cooking apples	42p
30ml/2 tablespoons demerara sugar	4p
150ml/5 fl oz water	

Method

1   Make the pastry using the method outlined in Basic Essentials (page 34). Use three-quarters of the pastry to line an oven-proof pie dish and bake blind at 170°C/325°F (Gas Mark 3) for 8–10 minutes.
2   For the filling, rinse, quarter and core the apples. Slice them into the pastry-lined dish, sprinkle them with sugar and add the water.
3   Cover with a lid made from the remaining pastry. Make a small hole in the centre and brush the pastry with milk.
4   Bake on the middle shelf of the oven at 180°C/350°F (Gas Mark 4) for 30 minutes until the pastry is golden brown and the fruit well cooked. Serve with custard, cream, ice cream or yogurt.

Approximate cost of ingredients: 78p

Note:
The following combinations make good fruit pies: blackberry and apple, apple and raisins with cinnamon, rhubarb and lemon, apple, gooseberry and banana.

Wholefruit Cake

Ingredients	*Approximately*
170g/6 oz demerara sugar	24p
85g/3 oz margarine	9p
455g/1 lb dried fruit	60p
5ml/1 teaspoon mixed spice	
5ml/1 level teaspoon bicarbonate of soda	
570ml/1 pint water	
2 eggs	16p
455g/1 lb self-raising wholemeal flour	16p

Method

1 Put all the ingredients except the eggs and flour, into a saucepan. Add the 570ml/1 pint water and bring to the boil. Reduce the heat and simmer gently for 15 minutes then leave to cool for 25 minutes.
2 When cool, beat in the eggs and gradually stir in the flour.
3 Turn into a greased 25cm/10-inch tin and bake at 170°C/ 325°F (Gas Mark 3) for 2 hours or until a knife inserted into the middle comes out clean.

Approximate cost of ingredients: £1.25

Note:
This recipe doubles as a party cake with the addition of lemon icing made with lemon juice and icing sugar.

● To freshen stale cake put the cake in a pudding basin, cover with a lid or plate and steam for 30 minutes.

Flapjacks

Ingredients	Approximately
140g/5 oz margarine	15p
85g/3 oz demerara sugar	12p
15ml/1 tablespoon molasses or black treacle	9p
225g/8 oz rolled oats	16p

Method

1 Melt the margarine, sugar and molasses slowly in a large saucepan. Add the oats and spread onto an oiled, shallow 25cm/10-inch round baking tin and bake at 190°C/375°F (Gas Mark 5) for 20–25 minutes.

2 Mark into squares while still hot and remove from the tin when cold.

Approximate cost of ingredients: 52p

Wholemeal Scones

Ingredients	Approximately
680g/1½ lb wholemeal flour	24p
5ml/1 rounded teaspoon baking powder	
2.5ml/½ teaspoon salt	
200g/7 oz margarine	21p
200g/7 oz sultanas	26p
570ml/1 pint milk and water mixed	20p
Beaten egg, to glaze	

Method

1 Mix the flour, baking powder and salt. Rub in the margarine until the mixture is like breadcrumbs.

2 Add the sultanas and the milk mixture and stir to make a soft dough. Knead lightly on a floured surface to make a ball then roll out to 2cm/¾ inch thick and cut out about 10 rounds.

3 Transfer them to a greased baking tray, brush with beaten egg and bake at 180°C/350°F (Gas Mark 4) for 20 minutes.

Approximate cost of ingredients: 91p

Oat Cookies

Ingredients	*Approximately*
115g/4 oz margarine	12p
85g/3 oz demerara sugar	12p
115g/4 oz crunchy peanut butter	24p
115g/4 oz oats	8p
115g/4 oz self-raising wholemeal flour	5p
55g/2 oz raisins	8p
5ml/1 teaspoon bicarbonate of soda	

Method
1 Melt the margarine and sugar in a saucepan. Stir in the peanut butter, oats, flour, raisins and bicarbonate of soda and mix well.
2 Place spoonfuls of the mixture onto a greased baking sheet. Bake in the middle of the oven at 180°C/350°F (Gas Mark 4) for 20 minutes.

Approximate cost of ingredients: 69p

Exemplary Menus for 4 Weeks

It may be helpful at this point to explain that should you overshoot the weekly figure of £28 in the initial weeks, this need not mean a failure to budget successfully. If, for example, in the first week you should decide on Mulligatawny Soup for Wednesday's lunch, which entails purchase of a pack of cayenne pepper for 50p, only to use a penny's worth, you'll not need to buy any more cayenne pepper for a month of Sundays, and your weekly budget will gradually balance out.

A good way to keep within budget is to use up any ingredients you may already have in, for example, if you have plenty of carrots, lettuce, tomato and cucumber and about 340g/¾ lb of lentils, you could make a Lentil Flan. You would only need to buy onions, garlic, lemon, watercress and potatoes to make Lentil Flan with baked potatoes and Simple Salad.

- Shopping is easier if menus are planned several days or a week in advance.

- The purchase of concentrated fruit juice proves convenient as it takes up less space in your fridge than bulky cartons (1 litre easily serves our family for a week), and carton juice is usually made from concentrated juice.

Week One

	Breakfasts	Lunches	Dinners	Total
Sun	Miser's Muesli for 4, **72p**	Mackerel Pâté 55p 12 slices wholemeal bread 24p, **79p**	Roast Chicken £2.80, Baked Potatoes 20p, Salad 60p, **£3.60**	**£5.11**
Mon	Boiled eggs 32p and wholemeal toast (8 slices) 16p, **48p**	Sardines on toast (12 slices) **£1.20**	Lentil Flan £1.40 Baked Potatoes 20p Salad 60p, **£2.20**	**£3.88**
Tue	Boiled eggs and wholemeal toast **48p**	Baked beans (1 lb 4 oz/567g tin) 58p wholemeal toast (8 slices) 16p, **74p**	Spaghetti Neapolitan £1.31, Salad 60p, **£1.91**	**£3.13**
Wed	Boiled eggs and wholemeal toast **48p**	Cream Mushroom Soup 94p, wholemeal bread 16p, **£1.10**	Blackeye Beanburgers £1.01, Baked Potatoes 20p, Salad 60p, **£1.81**	**£3.39**
Thu	Cornmeal Pudding **49p**	Pilchards on toast (12 slices) **76p**	Mexican Beans £1.95, Baked potatoes 20p, Salad 60p, **£2.75**	**£4.00**
Fri	Oat Porridge **50p**	Humous Spread on wholemeal bread (12 slices) with salad 10p, **73p**	Spicy Mackerel £1.71, Brown rice 40p, Salad 60p, **£2.71**	**£3.94**
Sat	Boiled eggs and wholemeal toast **48p**	Sweet Pancakes with honey/lemon/banana **86p**	Cheese & Vegetable Pie £1.80, Baked Potatoes 20p, Salad 60p **£2.60**	**£3.94**
				£27.39

Week Two

	Breakfasts	Lunches	Dinners	Total
Sun	4 boiled eggs 32p, toast (8 slices) 16p, **48p**	Redbean Salad 98p, bread (8 slices) 16p, **£1.14**	Chicken Curry £2.00, Boiled Rice 40p, Salad 60p, **£3.00**	**£4.62**
Mon	Oat Porridge for 4 **50p**	Lentil Soup **£1.00** bread 16p, **£1.16**	Popeye Pasties £1.68, Baked Potatoes 20p, Salad 60p, **£2.48**	**£4.14**
Tue	Oat Porridge **50p**	Cheese Omelette 74p, wholemeal bread 16p, **90p**	Quick Quiche £1.35, Baked Potatoes 20p, Salad 60p, **£2.15**	**£3.55**

Wed Oat Porridge 50p	Humous Spread on bread (12 slices) 73p	Potato Pie £1.18 Salad 60p, £1.78	£3.21
Thu Oat Porridge 50p	Cream Mushroom Soup 94p, wholemeal bread (8 slices) 16p, £1.10	Toad in the Hole £1.46, Baked Potatoes 20p, Salad 60p, £2.26	£3.86
Fri Oat Porridge 50p	Mushroom, Onion and Beansprout Pan- cakes 83p	Baked Mackerel £2.00, Baked potatoes 20p, Salad 60p, £2.80	£4.13
Sat Boiled eggs and wholemeal toast 48p	Macaroni Salad 86p wholemeal bread (4 slices) 8p, 94p	Cowboy Beans £1.35, Baked Potatoes 20p, Salad 60p, £2.15	£3.57
			£27.08

Week Three

	Breakfasts	Lunches	Dinners	Total
Sun	4 boiled eggs 32p, 8 slices wholemeal toast 16p, 48p	Mackerel Salad £1.58, wholemeal bread 16p, £1.74	Chicken & Vegetable Pie £2.25, Baked Potatoes 20p, Salad 60p, £3.05	£5.27
Mon	Cornmeal Porridge for 4 73p	Cream Cheese and Spinach Pancakes £1.24	Redbean Burgers £1.01, Baked Potatoes 20p Salad 60p, £1.81	£3.78
Tue	Cornmeal Porridge 73p	Minestrone Soup 60p, wholemeal bread 16p, 76p	Rice 'n' Peas £1.59, Baked Potatoes 20p, Salad 60p, £2.39	£3.88
Wed	Cornmeal Pudding 49p	Yorkshire Omelette 85p wholemeal bread 16p, £1.01	Sweet 'n' Sour Pork £1.00, Brown Rice 40p, Sauté Vegetables 70p, Salad 60p, £2.70	£4.20
Thu	Cornmeal Porridge 73p	Mushroom Onion and Beansprout Pan- cakes 83p	Spring Vegetable Soup 87p, wholemeal bread (8 slices) 16p, Humble Crumble 86p, Custard 30p, £2.04	£3.75
Fri	Cornmeal Porridge 73p	Baked beans (1lb 4 oz/ 567g tin) 58p, who- lemeal toast 16p, 74p	Spaghetti Bolognaise £1.87, Salad 60p, £2.47	£3.94

Sat	4 boiled eggs and wholemeal toast (8 slices) 48p	Redbean Salad 98p wholemeal bread 16p, **£1.14**	Lentil Flan £1.74, Baked Potatoes 20p, Salad 60p **£2.54**	**£4.16**

£28.98

Week Four

	Breakfasts	Lunches	Dinners	Total
Sun	4 boiled eggs and wholemeal toast (8 slices 48p	Taramasalata 45p wholemeal bread (12 slices) 24p, salad 10p, **79p**	Roast Chicken £2.80, Baked Potatoes 20p, Salad 60p, **£3.60**	**£4.87**
Mon	Miser's Muesli 72p	Cream Celery Soup 94p, wholemeal bread (8 slices) 16p, **£1.10**	Blackeye Bean-burgers £1.01 Baked Potatoes 20p Salad 60p, **£1.81**	**£3.63**
Tue	Miser's Muesli 72p	Baked beans 58p wholemeal toast (8 slices) 16p, **74p**	Lentil Loaf £1.05, Baked Potatoes 20p, Salad 60p, **£1.85**	**£3.31**
Wed	Miser's Muesli 72p	Tomato Bouillon 64p, wholemeal bread (8 slices) 16p, **80p**	Baked Mackerel £2.00, Baked Potatoes 20p, Salad 60p, **£2.80**	**£4.32**
Thu	Miser's Muesli 72p	Welsh Rarebit £1.06, wholemeal toast (12 slices) 24p, **£1.30**	Vegetable Curry £1.18, Brown Rice 40p, Salad 60p, **£2.18**	**£4.20**
Fri	Toast Cereal 43p	Pilchards on toast (12 slices), **76p**	Quick Quiche £1.35, Baked Potatoes 20p, Salad 60p, **£2.15**	**£3.34**
Sat	Bread Cereal 59p	Sweet Pancakes with honey/lemon/banana, **86p**	Fish Cakes £1.40, Baked Potatoes 20p, Salad 60p, **£2.20**	**£3.65**

£27.32

Index